This is
Citizenship 1

This is
Citizenship 1

Julia Fiehn Terry Fiehn

In memory of Ida Fiehn.

Although every effort has been made to ensure that website addresses are correct at time of going to press, Hodder Education cannot be held responsible for the content of any website mentioned in this book. It is sometimes possible to find a relocated web page by typing in the address of the home page for a website in the URL window of your browser.

Hachette Livre UK's policy is to use papers that are natural, renewable and recyclable products and made from wood grown in sustainable forests. The logging and manufacturing processes are expected to conform to the environmental regulations of the country of origin.

Orders: please contact Bookpoint Ltd, 130 Milton Park, Abingdon, Oxon OX14 4SB. Telephone: (44) 01235 827720. Fax: (44) 01235 400454. Lines are open 9.00–5.00, Monday to Saturday, with a 24-hour message answering service. Visit our website at www.hoddereducation.co.uk

Cover photo: © Gary Jochim/Superstock
Illustrations by Karen Donnelly, Richard Duszczak, Peter Greenwood, Tony Jones, Janek Matysiak, Chris Pavely, Chris Rothero, Steve Smith
Designed in 11/14pt Frutiger by Stephen Rowling/Springworks
Printed in Italy

A catalogue record for this title is available from the British Library

ISBN: 978 0340 947 098

Other titles in the series

This is Citizenship 1 Pupil's Book: 978 0340 947098
This is Citizenship 1 Teacher's Resource: 978 0340 947140
This is Citizenship 1 Dynamic Learning: 978 0340 947111

This is Citizenship 2 Pupil's Book: 978 0340 947128
This is Citizenship 2 Teacher's Resource: 978 0340 947135
This is Citizenship 2 Dynamic Learning: 978 0340 947142

This is Citizenship 3 Pupil's Book: 978 0340 947159
This is Citizenship 3 Teacher's Resource: 978 0340 947166
This is Citizenship 3 Dynamic Learning: 978 0340 947173

Contents

The Publishers would like to thank the following for permission to reproduce copyright material:

Photo credits
p.33 © Mauro Rinaldi/Alamy; **p.38** © Design Pics Inc./Alamy; **p.39** Terry Fiehn; **p.40** © terry harris just greece photo library/Alamy; **p.48** *t* Terry Fiehn, *m* © Simon Vine/Alamy, *b* Terry Fiehn; **p.56** © face to face Bildagentur GmbH/Alamy; **p.58** *t* Rex Features, *bl* © Justin Kase zonez/Alamy, *br* Martin Bond/Science Photo Library; **p.63** SAM PANTHAKY/AFP/Getty Images; **p.66** *tl* Argus/Hartmut Schwarzbach/Still Pictures, *tr* © vario images GmbH & Co.KG/Alamy, *bl* ODD ANDERSEN/AP/PA Photos, *br* Ron Giling/Still Pictures; **p.67** *tl* Martin Harvey/Getty Images, *tr* © Rainer Kzonsek/ DAS FOTOARCHIV/Still Pictures, *bl* SIMON MAINA/AFP/Getty Images, *br* © Indiapicture/Alamy; **p.71** © Frans Lemmens/Still Pictures; **p.72** © Eddie Gerald /Alamy; **p.74** *l* © argus/Mike Schroeder/Still Pictures, *m* © Paul A. Souders/CORBIS, *r* Nigel Dickinson/Still Pictures; **p.75** Terry Fiehn; **p.76** Fairtrade Foundation; **p.78** Ricardo Mazalan/Associated Press/PA; **p.79** "African women's project in Sudan/Dafur" on page 78 is reproduced from www.oxfam.org.uk with the permission of Oxfam GB, Oxfam House, John Smith Drive, Cowley, Oxford OX4 2JY, UK Oxfam GB does not necessarily endorse any text or activities that accompany the materials.

Acknowledgements
p.17 'No man is an island' written by John Donne **p.33** The Scout Association, for quotation from the Scout Association official website; **p.54** Waste Watch, Leading Environmental Charity, www.wastewatch.org.uk, for Wacky waste facts from www.wasteonline.com; **p.68** New Internationalist, for Case study 1 from *New Internationalist*; **p.68** CAFOD, for Case study 3 by Chris Holt; **p.69** UNICEF, for The United Nations Convention on the Rights of the Child (1989); **p.76** *Fairtrade logo* Fairtrade Foundation; **p.77** OXFAM Publishing, Oxfam GB, Oxfam House, John Smith Drive, Cowley, Oxford OX4 2JY, for a quotation from www.oxfam.org.uk, **p.79** *Red Cross/Red Crescent logos* Reproduced by permission of the International Federation of Red Cross and Red Crescent Societies, *Oxfam logo* Reproduced from www.oxfam.org.uk with the permission of Oxfam GB, Oxfam House, John Smith Drive, Cowley, Oxford OX4 2JY, UK Oxfam GB does not necessarily endorse any text or activities that accompany the materials, *Christian Aid logo* With kind permission of Christian Aid www.christianaid.org.uk; *WaterAid logo* Reproduced by permission of WaterAid.

Grateful thanks to the staff and pupils of Bishop's Hatfield Girls' School and especially to Sue Carter. Thanks to the pupils of Gallions School, Newham and especially Mark Chapman.

In a fair society, all people should expect to have basic rights and to be treated equally. Having rights does not mean that you can behave just as you like. You have to consider how your actions affect other people if our society is to be a pleasant place to live. Groups develop rules to ensure that people can get on together. However, it can be difficult to apply rules and make decisions so that everybody feels they have been treated fairly.

KEY WORDS

rules

fairness

rights

responsibility

Assessing your progress
In this section you will be assessing how well you can:

- express opinions
- give reasons for or justify your opinions
- listen to and take account of other people's views
- understand the issues.

You are part of a team visiting Planet Hoff to compare the way they run their schools with those on Earth. Schools on Hoff are well known for their excellent discipline.

People at Zap High School

There are four groups of people in Zap High School:

Knowers pass on their knowledge and skills to the Learners. They do not discipline the Learners.

Enforcers do not teach. They punish anyone who misbehaves in class or breaks the school rules. They keep records on the Learners, which the Learners are not allowed to see.

Learners are the school pupils.

Monitors are a small group of senior Learners chosen and trained by the Enforcers. They make sure that Learners obey the rules and make reports on those who break rules, e.g. dropping litter.

Rules and punishments at Zap High School

Zap High School is very strict. There are clear rules, which are never changed or discussed. The rules are pinned on the walls of the school and sent to every family.

Learners who break the rules are given punishments worked out on a points system. For example, talking in class is 4 points, and rudeness to a Knower is 10 points. So, if a Learner talks in class **and** is rude, the punishment is worth 14 points.

Here are some of the rules and punishments:

Rules	Points
Leaving doors open, leaving taps running	1
Dropping litter, running	2
Arriving late to class	3
Talking in class	4
Chewing, eating	5
Swearing	6
Rudeness to Knower	10

Points	Punishments
1	Standing still in middle of dining hall for 10 minutes during lunch
2	Writing 50 lines
3	Detention for 30 minutes after school
4	Letter home and detention for one hour
5	One stroke of cane on hand
10	Five strokes of cane on hand

If Learners build up too many points regularly, they receive 20 strokes of the cane and can be expelled from the school.

The Enforcers and the Monitors make sure the Learners follow the rules. Punishments are strictly applied by the Enforcers. The Learners have no say at all. They cannot appeal to anyone if they feel they have not been treated fairly.

Activity

1 a) What do you think is fair/unfair about the system of rules and punishments at Zap High School?
   b) Working in groups of three or four, decide on six things that Zap High School would need to change to make its rules fairer.

2 a) What are the similarities and differences between Zap High School and your own school?
   b) Which part of the Zap system would you like to see in your school? Why?

3 Do you think it is a good idea to have:
   a) Enforcers, separate from teachers, who discipline pupils who misbehave?
   b) Monitors – pupils who help make sure others follow the rules?

All groups of people develop rules – things you can and can't do – whether the group is a family, a group of friends, a youth club or a school. Some of the rules are formal and written down. Others are informal, but are still clearly understood by all the members of the group. There are usually consequences for those who break the rules.

Most schools have formal, written rules. These aim to keep order and protect the rights of everyone in the school.

1 In groups, think about your school rules. Which ones do you think are fair and which unfair? Decide which of the rules you would change if you could. Then justify your choice to the rest of the class.

– NO RUNNING IN CORRIDOR –

2 a) Who makes rules in schools?
  b) Should school pupils be involved in making school rules?

3 a) Work in pairs. One of you is 'X', the other is 'Y'.

• X writes the beginning of a story in which a rule is broken. Don't tell Y what you are writing.
• Y writes the end of a story which tells about how somebody is punished after he or she has broken a rule.
• X and Y swap stories.
• X writes the beginning of Y's story. Y writes the end of X's story.

  b) Choose some of the stories to read out in class.

4 Write down six rules that you think a school must have.

5 For each rule, decide what punishment a pupil should receive for breaking it and explain what the punishment should achieve.

6 Are punishments always the best way of stopping people breaking rules? What other solutions can you suggest?

NO EATING IN THE CLASSROOM ✗

Make your own class ground rules for discussions

In class discussions there is going to be disagreement and lots of people trying to talk at the same time. So you need some ground rules that everybody has to follow, and you should all be involved in making them.

Remember – everybody should be able to participate and get their views heard.

Activity

1 Working in pairs, draw up your list of rules. If you wish you can use the 'Starters' on the right.
2 When you have finished, join up with another pair and share what you have written. Try to create a list you can all agree on.
3 All the fours should then come together as a class and agree a set of rules.
4 Make posters of the agreed rules to display around the class.

STATEMENT STARTERS

A 'When we are discussing as a class, we should ...'

B 'When someone is talking, we should ...'

C 'If someone disagrees with what someone else has said, ...'

D 'If there are different views in the class, we could ...'

E 'Decisions could be made by ...'

F 'If we don't understand what someone has said, we should ...'

G 'If someone breaks the rules, ...'

H 'If someone is unkind, ...'

If you were the teacher …

It is not quite so easy applying rules as it might appear. It can be difficult to be fair to everyone. Look at Jenny Bennett's day as a teacher and all the things she has to deal with. Could you do better?

Jenny Bennett arrived just on time for school as she had been up part of the night with her 5-year-old daughter. But she had still got in on time for registration. However, Mike Drake in her tutor group had not arrived on time again. She knew he had a difficult journey by bus, but the headteacher had recently stressed that there could be no excuses for being late.

Decision 1
She gave Mike a late detention.

At registration Susan told her that she had forgotten to bring her money for the trip to the rap music session that all the pupils had been looking forward to.

Decision 2
She said that Susan could not go. Susan was upset and said she would bring the money the next day, but Mrs Bennett said she would stick to her decision.

After registration Jenny went off to teach her first lesson, an English GCSE class. As she was talking to the class, she spotted Jason sending a text message on his mobile phone.

Decision 3
She took Jason's phone away and said she would give it to his head of year. One of his parents would have to come to the school to collect it. It was a strict rule of the school that mobile phones should not be used in lessons.

Work in pairs. Read what Mrs Bennett did through the day. Whenever she made a decision, you have to decide whether she was right, partly right, or wrong. Be prepared to say why and what you would have done.

Fortunately the next lesson passed without incident and Jenny went off to get a cup of tea at break time. As she came round the corner she saw an older boy pinning a younger one against the wall. The younger one appeared to be crying. She questioned them about what they were doing, but they said they were just mucking around.

Decision 4
She decided to do nothing and went off to have her cup of tea.

In the lesson before lunch, her Year 7 class kept on being noisy. Some of the pupils were making noises when her back was turned, but she could not pin down who the troublemakers were. After one warning …

Decision 5
She told them she would keep them in for ten minutes at lunch and add on five minutes if the disturbance happened again. It did, so she kept them for fifteen minutes, even though the pupils complained that they would lose their place in the dinner rota and there would not be much food left.

Jenny grabbed a quick lunch and got her lesson materials ready for the afternoon. Afternoon registration was quick and easy. But the first lesson with her Year 9 English class did not go so smoothly. In the middle of the lesson Nissa Ahmed suddenly jumped up and threw her schoolbag at John Jenks, cutting his face. She said that he had made a racist statement about her family and religious beliefs.

Decision 6
Mrs Bennett hauled John out of the class and sent him to the deputy headteacher who deals with racist incidents. John was sent home with a letter to his parents at the end of the afternoon.

However, the rest of the class was unsettled. Some pupils told Mrs Bennett that John did not make the remarks and that Nissa was angry with him because he had dumped her best friend and she wanted to get him into trouble.

Decision 7
Mrs Bennett ignored their comments.

The final school lesson pips sounded. It had been a long day.

It was the last lesson of the day. Jenny was relaxed because she was teaching her Year 12 class. But two of them had not handed in their essays. This had been a continual problem with these two pupils over several weeks.

Decision 8
She told them that if their essays were not on her desk first thing in the morning, she would recommend that they were dropped from the course.

DISCUSS

1 How far did you agree with Mrs Bennett's decisions?
2 What decisions did you find difficult?
3 Why do you think it is difficult to apply rules so that they are fair to everybody?

1.3 It's not fair!

People often say 'It's not fair!' when they mean 'It's not what I want.' It is important to understand what fairness is. Most of us like to think that we are fair to other people, and we want to be treated fairly ourselves.

Some people would say that, in order to be fair, we must:

- treat people equally
- not favour particular people
- not discriminate against particular people
- be open-minded and consider all the facts and viewpoints before coming to a decision
- be sure that punishments are not too harsh or too lenient.

The trouble is that it is not always easy to judge what is fair, as you can see from the cartoon strip 'Sam's Bad Day'.

Activity

1. Read the cartoon strip. Then answer these questions with a partner.
   a) What do you think of each of the things that happened to Sam?
   b) Were the punishments fair?
   c) Who was at fault, if anyone?
   d) What could Sam do?
2. Now discuss the same questions as a class.
3. In pairs, draw a storyboard of three pictures that shows a fair/unfair situation like the ones here. The subject could be:
   a) some school pupils messing around on a bus, which results in all of them getting thrown off
   b) buying an MP3 player that gets damaged and won't work, but the shop won't give you your money back
   c) one of your own choice.
   Swap your storyboard with another pair and discuss the situation in their storyboard with your partner. Some could be presented to the rest of the class.

Sam's Bad Day

The batteries in the alarm clock are dead. Sam oversleeps.

Today is the last day to pay for the Geography trip.

Some of the pupils mess about in Geography.

Sam arrives home. It's been a very bad day. Can it get worse?

Sam misses the bus and drops some money.

The teacher takes Sam's name. Detention tomorrow.

FAIR OR UNFAIR?

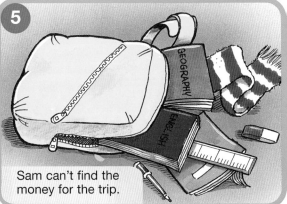

Sam can't find the money for the trip.

I'm sorry. If you haven't got the money today, you can't go on the trip.

Sam can't go on the trip.

FAIR OR UNFAIR?

The teacher keeps the whole class in for break. Sam misses the drama meeting.

Sam can't be in the drama production. All the parts have gone.

I'm sorry. All the parts are gone. You're too late.

FAIR OR UNFAIR?

Mum wants Sam to pick up the baby tomorrow, but Sam can't because of the detention.

Sam is grounded for getting three detentions this month.

FAIR OR UNFAIR?

Who will go to the TV studio?

Being fair is never easy. How would you reach a fair decision in the following example?

The problem

A class has entered a national competition which involved researching and designing posters and a website on the theme of 'Reducing Waste'. The whole class put together a folder on their project and it was sent off to the competition organisers. The prize is a visit to a TV studio where their work will be shown on television.

Excellent news! The class has been invited to the TV studio along with several other schools to show their work on waste reduction on children's television. But ... only six children from the class can attend. If you were in charge, how would you decide who should go?

Activity

Read statements A–L. Decide which ones should be taken into account when making the decision about who should go. Put them in order of importance.

A Some pupils worked very hard, but did not produce much work that went into the class folder.

B Two pupils did a lot of the work at home using their parents' computers and colour printers.

C One pupil is very unhappy at the moment because of problems at home and it would really cheer her up.

E A group of pupils did a lot of work, but they have been misbehaving in some of their other lessons and are on report.

D Several pupils do not have smart school uniforms.

F Three pupils came to see you privately and begged to be allowed to go because they want to be on television.

G One pupil worked fairly hard on the project and missed a previous school treat because he was very ill. He is better now.

H A disagreement has been going on for some time between two pupils. An outing together might help them make up.

I The mother of one of the pupils was very interested in the competition and came in to class to help out.

J Two pupils have done a lot of excellent work, as usual. They have won prizes before because they are very clever.

K One pupil, who has produced some good work, suffers badly from asthma and might be ill if she gets too excited.

L It would be good to have equal numbers of boys and girls.

DISCUSS

1 a) How difficult did you find it to decide on the order of importance?

b) Which of the statements should be taken into account? Why?

c) Which ones should not be taken into account? Why?

d) Are there any other ways in which the choice could be made? What are they?

2 a) Why do we get so angry when we think we have been treated unfairly?

b) Do you agree with people who say, 'Tough! Life *is* unfair, you will just have to put up with it'?

What's the fairest way to give pupils places in secondary schools?

Fairness is important in society, but not everybody can get what they want. There are times when a number of people want the same things and this can lead to conflict and arguments. You have to find a way of resolving these in a fair way. One hot issue that comes up every year is how primary school pupils get places in secondary schools. What's the fairest way of sorting this out?

Recently in Brighton it was suggested that the best way to give primary pupils 'fair and equal access' to secondary schools might be a lottery. Here is how it might work:

- The city is divided up into six large areas called 'catchment areas' which have one or more secondary schools in them.
- Pupils apply to go to a school in the catchment area they live in.
- If lots of pupils want to go to a particular school and there are not enough places, then all of their names go into a lottery. A computer picks the lucky names at random.
- The pupils who do not get into the school will have to go to another school where there are places. These might be a long way away.

In the present system in Brighton, pupils go to the school nearest them. Some parents in Brighton are in favour of the scheme and some against. Here are some of the points they have made:

> **School places decided by lottery**

> *A In the present system, richer parents buy houses near good schools to make sure their children get in. That's not fair on others.*

> *B Children might not get into the school they live next to and then have to travel a long way to another school. You could have lots of children criss-crossing the city, travelling miles. This is not only ridiculous but it is bad for the environment.*

> *C At least a lottery will give an equal chance for everybody who lives in the area to get into a particular school.*

> *D The boundaries of the catchment area may cut some families off from sending their children to the school nearest to them. It might be in a different catchment area.*

> *E Parents with several children might end with all their children at different schools.*

> *F Parents fiddle most systems at present. But you would not be able to cheat in a lottery system – it will be fairer.*

Here are some of the main ways in which places are sorted out.

Pupils get places according to their **distance** from the school, so those who are closest get in.

Pupils get places because they live in the **catchment area** around the school. This may be quite a small area in cities or a very large one in the countryside.

Schools select pupils by **ability**. They may select pupils of high ability or they may choose pupils so that they have a range of ability in the school, i.e. equal numbers of pupils in Band 1 (highest), Band 2 and Band 3.

Some schools are **faith** schools. Pupils are able to go to these schools because they and their parents are Catholics, Jewish, Muslim, members of the Church of England or followers of another religion. Usually they have to show that they attend their places of worship regularly or are serious about their faith.

Pupils get places because they have **siblings** (brothers and sisters) in the school already. They are allowed in before others get a chance.

Some schools run a **combination** of these methods. For example, one school may select 20 per cent of pupils by ability, give places to siblings of current pupils, and the rest of the places according to those who live nearest the school.

Activity

Work in small groups.
1 How do you think the people listed below might be affected by the decision about which children go to certain secondary schools?
 • pupils
 • parents
 • pupil's friends
 • teachers (primary and secondary)
 • other people you can think of.
Think about
a) if pupils get a place in the school they wanted
b) if pupils do not get a place.

2 Divide a page into two columns. In one column, put the arguments for the catchment and lottery system and, in the other, put the arguments against. Use the comments in the white quote boxes on page 12 and your own ideas.
3 Using the information in the boxes above, decide what you think is the fairest way of choosing pupils for school places. You must give reasons for your opinions.
4 Your group should present its opinions to the whole class, and there can be a class discussion of different views.
5 Why is it so difficult to sort out this issue so that everybody feels they have been treated fairly?

1.4 What rights should all children have?

Children often feel that adults stop them from doing things they have a right to do. Adults say that they are protecting the child or looking after the child's interests. Some adults think that children do not have rights at all and that they are not able to decide matters for themselves.

Activity

1 Think of two or three occasions when an adult stopped you doing something you felt you had a right to do. Discuss the events in class.
2 What rights should all children have? Read the speech bubbles on these pages with a partner. Note down the rights that you think are really important. Note the ones you do not think are important or can't decide about. You could write them in a table like the one below. The first one has been done for you.

It is important that children should have the right to ...	It is not very important that children should have the right to ...	Children should NOT have the right to ...
free education		

A I should have the right to free education.

B I should have the right to go to bed when I want to.

C I should be able to get enough food to keep me healthy.

D I should have the right to stay with my family or the people who love me and want to look after me.

E I should have the right to drink alcohol.

F There should be times when I can play and relax.

G I should be able to go out and stay out until I decide it's time to come home.

H I should have the right to work to earn money to help my family.

I Adults should not bully me, beat me or abuse me in any way.

J Adults should listen to my views when they make a decision that will affect my life.

L I should have the right to decide what I learn at school.

K I should have the right to eat sweets when I want to.

N I should be able to watch whatever I like on television.

M I should have the right to special care and education if I am disabled.

O I should be allowed to develop my abilities and talents to the fullest.

DISCUSS

Discuss these questions as a whole class:
a) Which rights were you not sure about and why?
b) Which did you think were really important rights?
c) Which were not so important?
d) Which should children *not* have a right to?
e) Which other rights would you add to the ones you have said were important?

P I should have the right to use a credit card.

1.5 No man is an island ...

People expect to have rights, but do they expect to have responsibilities? We all have a responsibility to make sure that we don't put ourselves and other people in danger. But what other kinds of responsibility do people have towards each other, and how do we decide which are the most important?

Grandparents

Friends

Neighbours

Teachers

Activity

1 Think about the people on this list. Who would come first for you if they were in difficulty? Put the list in order of your priority and explain your decisions.

Elderly people you don't know

Strangers of your own age

Brothers/sisters

Yourself

Parents

People living far away in other countries

2 Now look at the following situations. Would any of these change the way you think about your responsibilities to different people, and the order you placed them in above?

You really want to buy a new CD, but you have been moved by the plight of people across the other side of the world involved in a terrible disaster. You could donate the money to help them.

Your friends have asked you to join them at a party. It will be a real laugh. However, it is your gran's 70th birthday, and she is looking forward to seeing all of her family.

Your teacher is counting on you to help paint the set for the school production after school today. You are good at art, you like the teacher and you promised you would. However, your mum has been asked out for an early evening drink and says she needs you to look after your baby brother.

You are out with a group of friends when you meet a young boy you don't know. One of your friends trips him up on purpose and he hurts his leg. His things spill out over the floor and all his money falls out of his pocket. Your friends walk off laughing, but the boy asks you for help.

Your older brother likes to tag walls. An elderly neighbour has just had a new garden wall built. He is really pleased with it and is not very well off. Your brother says he is going to spray the new wall with his tag. You could try to persuade him not to, since you and your brother get on very well.

You have seen a pair of trainers that you really like, but you have also discovered that the people who make them work very long hours for little money. Do you refuse to buy the trainers and send a letter to the company to tell them why, or do you buy them and think it's only one pair and what you do does not make any difference?

DISCUSS

1 How do we decide who to put first in difficult situations like these?
2 Why is it sometimes difficult to decide against our friends?
3 Do you think that you have any responsibility towards other people who you don't know?
4 What do you think the expression in the poem 'No man is an island' means? Do you agree with it?

No man is an island,
Entire of itself.
Each is a piece of the
 continent,
A part of the main.

John Donne

In the park

dog owner

children

park keeper

mother and toddler

At the shopping centre

CLOGGS

CLOTHES 4 U

COFF

shopkeepers

shoppers

children

shopping centre manager

security guards

In the street

It is easy to say that other people are responsible for things that happen, and people often don't accept responsibility for their own actions. Who do you think is responsible in these scenes?

Activity

Work in groups of three or four. For each scene, discuss the following questions:

a) What responsibilities do the named people in your scene have in that situation or place?

b) What bad/dangerous outcomes could be the result of what some people are doing/not doing?

c) Do you think some people are more responsible than others? Choose the two people from each scene who you think have the greatest responsibility for what is going on, and say why.

d) Compare the opinions of different groups about the responsibilities of people in the scenes. See if other people's views change your opinions.

motorcyclist

car driver

community support officer

girls crossing road

old lady

cyclist

councillors

YOUTH CENTRE

CLOSED

bus driver

mother and toddlers

young people

boy

people in queue

Taking responsibility

Taking responsibility isn't always about *not* doing irresponsible things and just being 'good'.

Sometimes it involves taking positive action yourself, or trying to persuade other people to do something, to make things better for everyone.

Try this quiz on your own. In each of the situations you could choose to do nothing, or take action yourself, or persuade someone else to take some action. You might come up with something better that could be done. If so, note this down. In some of the situations, it might not be safe or appropriate for you to do *anything*.

Compare your answers with those of a partner.

1 There is broken glass under the swings in the local park. You realise that small children could be hurt. Do you:
a) avoid the glass yourself and do nothing?
b) find an adult who works in the park and tell them?
c) pick up the glass and put it in the bin?
d) do something else? ....

2 You know that there is a bullying problem in your class. You are not involved yourself, but you know what is going on and you don't like it. Do you:
a) ignore it because it's none of your business?
b) tell the class teacher who the bullies are?
c) raise the general topic of bullying during tutorial and discuss a class strategy to deal with it?
d) do something else? ....

3 There are lots of old people living on your estate. Some of them seem quite frightened of young people, like you and your friends. Do you:
a) feel bad, but do nothing?
b) talk to them occasionally, in a friendly way, so they don't feel threatened?
c) suggest to the local day centre that they organise some regular meetings for old and young people to meet and talk?
d) do something else? ....

4 Someone has written some racist graffiti on a wall near your school. Do you:
a) ignore it – it's offensive, but there's nothing you can do?
b) wash the graffiti off yourself or scribble over it?
c) complain to the local council and ask for it to be removed?
d) do something else? ....

5 You have been learning about the problem of waste and rubbish, and you think more people should recycle their glass, tins, paper, plastic, etc. The school grounds are full of such litter. Do you:
a) do nothing – it's not your responsibility?
b) take your own litter to the recycling bins?
c) suggest to the school council that it campaigns for recycling bins in school to stop litter-dropping?
d) do something else? ....

6 An article in your local newspaper reports wrongly on an incident that happened in your school and puts the school in a bad light. Do you:
a) get cross, but do nothing?
b) email or write to the paper to complain?
c) start a petition in the school to support a letter requesting that the newspaper prints an apology?
d) do something else? ....

7 You are concerned about child labour in other parts of the world and have done a project on it in school. Do you:
a) give your project in to your teacher and do nothing else?
b) decide to boycott certain goods which may have been made by children?
c) help produce an exhibition on child labour and ask that it be displayed in the school, to tell others about it?
d) do something else? ....

8 You are not happy with the way that the school council works. It doesn't seem to get anything done. Do you:
a) have nothing to do with the school council?
b) stand as the class representative yourself?
c) persuade the council to have an open meeting at which criticisms can be discussed?
d) do something else? ....

DISCUSS

Discuss the responses of the whole class and think about each of these questions:
1 In which situations could something be done?
2 When is it best to take action yourself, and when should others take the action?
3 Are there any other situations like this? Think of two more.

How much say should pupils have in what happens in school?

Some people think that you learn useful skills and feel that you belong if you are allowed to voice your views and be listened to. Others believe that children do not have enough experience of life to be able to influence important decisions.

Activity

Think about each of the following six situations. Decide which three pupils should have a say in. Comment on why you chose these three rather than the others?

Now look at the eight skills described. You might need to use different skills in the three chosen situations. Match the skills to the situations.

Situations

The school is to have a new headteacher. The job has been advertised and people have applied.

Should pupils be involved in choosing the headteacher? If so, how?

a) shortlisting
b) meeting applicants
c) interviewing

The school grounds are very scruffy, with litter blowing around, graffiti on the walls and nowhere to sit. Some money has been made available for improvements – new bins, a clean-up and some seating.

Should pupils be consulted about how the grounds can be kept in good condition?

Dinner time at the school is very chaotic. Too many people are trying to pass through the dining hall in too short a time. Some Year 7 pupils have worked out a plan that might improve things.

Should the headteacher listen and be persuaded to try out the plan?

There has always been a debate in the school about uniform. No one likes the existing one – the colours are drab and the styles old-fashioned. Some people think there should be no uniform at all; others think the uniform should be redesigned.

Should pupils be involved in making the decision by debating and voting?

All schools have a board of governors who oversee the running of the school. Some of the governors are parents or teachers who have been elected.

Should pupils be able to elect a pupil governor? They would probably only be able to listen and report back on meetings rather than make decisions.

The school is to be rebuilt on a new site and the new buildings will be opened in four years' time. There are some choices that have to be made about the improved facilities.

Should there be a pupil committee working with staff and the architect?

Skills

> Listening to different points of view

> Expressing a point of view and explaining it

> Asking sensible questions and following up things you don't understand

> Being able to say briefly what was said (summarising) and reporting back to others

> Finding out what other people think, and deciding what the majority view is

> Arguing a case

> Speaking on behalf of others and putting their views forward even if you don't agree with them yourself

> Negotiating – accepting compromises if reasonable

Ways of being involved in how the school is run

There are a number of different ways in which pupils can regularly make their views known and offer suggestions to change things:

- school councils (see pages 24–25)
- suggestion boxes
- notice boards
- chatrooms and blogs on the school website
- focus groups (where small groups of pupils are consulted on specific issues)
- whole school votes, through a show of hands in assembly, or a referendum with votes being put in a ballot box
- discussing what is going to be learned in subjects.

What do you think of each of these? Do they happen in your school? If not, which of these would you like to see in your school?

Who represents your views at school?

Most schools these days have some kind of school council, which is made up of elected pupil representatives. All the pupils in the school have the chance to stand for election to represent their class, their year group or their house.

School councils have a number of purposes:

- to help everyone in the school to feel responsible for what goes on there
- to improve relationships between teachers and pupils
- to help pupils get on better with each other
- to solve any problems in the school
- to build pupils' confidence by giving them a chance to speak in public
- to give pupils the skills needed to work in groups.

The elected members of the council meet regularly, sometimes with a teacher present and sometimes not. They discuss items that have been put on the agenda by pupils and staff. The council's decisions are written down and put forward to the headteacher, and sometimes the governors of the school.

DISCUSS

1 How is your school council organised?
2 How are members of the council selected? Do you think this is a fair way of choosing representatives?
3 Pick two of the 'purposes' of school councils that you think your council fulfils and say why.

School councils are run differently in different schools, and some work better than others. Here are some of the criticisms pupils have made of school councils:

A I'm not interested in the school council. It's boring and doesn't affect me.

B It's always the same kinds of pupils who get elected to the council – the clever and confident ones.

C Whatever the school council decides, the headteacher really makes the decisions. We can't change anything.

D We never hear what happens at council meetings. They don't tell the rest of us anything.

E The school council is a clique. They think they are the top dogs because the teachers consult them.

F I never manage to get my items on the agenda of the school council. Who decides what they talk about? Not me.

Activity

1 Work in small groups and discuss each of the statements above. How far is each one true of your school council?

2 If some of the statements are true, what could be done to change things?

3 a) As a class, discuss your ideas for improving the school council. Each group calls out one idea at a time. This should be written on the board. If an idea is put forward by more than one group, it should be ticked each time it is suggested.

b) Pick the three ideas that have the most ticks and hold a vote on which improvement is the most important. You can suggest this improvement to your school council representative, or you could write a letter to the school council from the class, asking for your ideas to go on the next agenda.

1.8 Taking part in a debate

Debating is a good way to explore all sides of a particular issue. Usually the issue is put in the form of a statement that people can argue about, e.g. 'It should be made illegal for parents to smack their children.' We call this a motion.

In the picture below, you can see the different roles people play in a debate. You are now going to debate the issue about smacking children. This is a good issue to discuss because the theme of this section is fairness, rights and responsibilities. Children have rights, as you discussed on pages 14–15. But parents are responsible for bringing up their children to behave well.

Activity

Arrange the classroom and agree the main speakers. Give them and others a chance to prepare their arguments. Use the statements here and on page 28 to get started. You should also do some research (see page 29).

I am arguing that parents should not smack their children for any reason, and so there should be a law against it. My reasons for saying this are …

People may think that the odd smack does not hurt a child, but it usually does not stop at this. Parents who hit …

The motion for the debate today is: 'This house believes that it should be made illegal for parents to smack their children.'

Chairperson

My role is to run and control the debate.

- I keep everybody in order.
- I start the debate by reading out the motion.
- I call people to speak and keep to time.
- I choose people from the audience to join in, taking people in turn for and against the motion.
- I try to make sure the debate is fair.
- At the end I take a vote on whether people are for or against the motion.

For the motion

Speaker 1

My role is to speak first *for* the motion.

- I make points to support the motion.
- I speak for 2–3 minutes.

Speaker 3

- I also speak for the motion.
- I speak for 2–3 minutes.

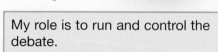

I cannot believe that the first speaker argues that a child should never be smacked. While we agree that children should not be hit hard, there are several occasions when a short sharp smack is the best thing for a child …

I agree with the first speaker, hitting children never …

My main point is that some small children are very naughty and won't listen to what their parents say, so a small smack …

We are talking here about it being made illegal to smack a child. That means that the police can arrest a parent, which is ridiculous. Think of what this might mean …

I am not totally against smacking, but parents should not be allowed to hit children around the head, because …

The audience

Our role is to listen and contribute to the debate.

- We listen to the speeches from both sides.
- We can ask the speakers questions.
- We can make our own short speeches or give our views.
- We can only join in when the chairperson says so.

Against the motion

Speaker 2

My role is to speak first *against* the motion.

- I make points which disagree with the motion.
- I speak for 2–3 minutes.

Speaker 4

- I also speak against the motion.
- I speak for 2–3 minutes.

Arguments for and against the motion: *It should be made illegal for parents to smack their children.*

Arguments for

A Children who are hit often grow up to be adults who hit their children.

B It's better to spend time talking to a child if he or she has done something wrong. Then they learn what they have done wrong.

D If you allow people to smack a child, some adults will always go too far and hit the child too hard.

I The only way we can be sure that parents don't hit children too hard is to stop them hitting children altogether.

K Children should have the same rights as adults. You wouldn't hit an adult if they made too much noise or ran around. So you shouldn't hit a child either.

L There are better ways to control children than to hit them. Some European countries like Austria and Sweden have made it illegal for parents to hit their children.

Arguments against

C If a child has hit someone else, it's important for the child to find out what it's like to be hit.

E A short, sharp smack corrects a small child much more quickly than hours of talking. They soon learn what's right or wrong.

F Small children don't understand what is said to them.

G I've been smacked and it didn't harm me. Parents are responsible for making sure children behave, so you can't take away one of the ways they can do this. Children would then be able to do what they liked.

H A law banning smacking would mean that the government and police are interfering in people's lives too much. Next there will be a law to tell us when to change our underpants.

J If you had a law, how would you prove parents were not hitting their child in their homes? This is too much interference in people's lives.

Developing your debating skills

You can improve your debating skills by practising them regularly. You can see below some of the areas you can work on.

Making points, giving reasons

In a debate you need to make points clearly and give reasons for your views.

We call this making an argument. Here is an example:

Point
It is wrong to test cosmetics on animals …

+

Reason
… because it causes them unnecessary suffering and pain.

Evidence
It is useful to support your argument with evidence.

> *One common test is for eye irritation where substances are dripped into rabbits' eyes to see what effects they cause. In rabbits this can lead to swollen eyelids, irritated eyes or even blindness. However, studies have shown that rabbits' eyes are different from those of human beings and that the tests cannot predict how human eyes will react to the substances.*

Activity

1 Give an example in the smacking debate when someone made a point and gave a reason to back up the point.
2 Work in pairs. Come up with a point and a reason about the following topics: school students should wear school uniforms, children under 11 should not be allowed out on the streets after 9 o'clock without an adult.

Researching

You have to understand the issue you are debating. This means finding out about it – collecting information and evidence to use in the debate. You can find out what other people think about the issue and reasons to back up your opinions. We can get information from a number of sources.

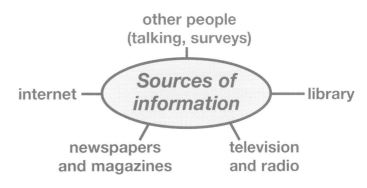

Activity

Which source(s) would be the best to find information on: current news events, opinions of people in your local area, experimentation on animals?

Reflection

How well do you think you're doing?
  Think back over the work you have done in Section 1.

Skills

- Draw a chart like the one below, and give yourself a grade from 1 to 5, where 1 is the lowest and 5 is the highest.
- Give evidence for your score and say how you could improve your skills.

Assessing your progress
In this section you will be assessing how well you can:

- express opinions
- give reasons for or justify your opinions
- listen to and take account of other people's views
- understand the issues.

How well can you ... ?	1	2	3	4	5	Evidence for your score?	How can you improve?
state your opinions (that is, 'express' them)							
give reasons for your opinions (that is, 'justify' them)							
listen to what other people say							
take account of other people's views when deciding what you think							
take part in whole class discussions							
take part in small group discussions							

Understanding

- Complete the following sentences:
  'I think fairness means …'
  'I think responsibilities are important because …'
- Talk to another pupil and discuss what you think was the most important thing you learned in this section.

Section 2
Communities and identities

What makes people feel that they belong?

GUTEN TAG Ahoj

Hello! Salut

नमस्ते Hej

Привет Bemmos días

DoBAR DAN

How do we get our identities?

What things do you like and dislike about your local community?

How can the environment of the community be improved?

How can we get involved and participate in improving things?

Being part of a community makes you feel that you belong. People usually belong to several different communities, and these help to shape our identity, the way we see ourselves. We all live in a local community – our neighbourhood – and we are also part of larger communities (like a city, a town or a county) where lots of different groups of people live. Sometimes people like the area they live in and feel they belong. Sometimes they don't like the area and feel that nobody cares about them and that they don't belong.

Assessing your progress
In this section you will be assessing how well you can:

- explain your opinions
- carry out research and undertake an enquiry
- represent other people's views
- think about ways of taking action to change things.

KEY WORDS

identity

community

culture

participation

2.1 Belonging to a community

People have different ideas about what a community is, and for many it is about belonging. Everyone needs to feel that he or she belongs.

Most people really feel they belong to the communities of people with whom they have something in common, such as their age, language, particular interests and hobbies, the job they do, or the religious beliefs they all share. Many people are part of, and feel they belong to, several communities that overlap – for example, school, friends, family and neighbours, clubs, ethnic group, place of worship.

Wei, Michael and Grace belong to several communities.

Neighbourhood

Wei

Facebook

School

Girl Guides

Second Life

Michael

Football

Youth club

Chess club

Grace

Sports centre

Friends

Church

Dance club

Activity

1 Draw a diagram to show the different communities you feel you belong to.
2 Are these all with people your own age, or do you share communities with people of different ages?
3 Create a list of all the different types of communities you can think of and then make a class list.

32

The Scouts

Scouts at World Jamboree in 2007

The Scouts are an interesting example of a community that works at different levels:

- **Local** – the Scout troop, where they train to do badges, learn skills like map reading and take part in organised events and adventurous activities. Every year most Scout troops go camping.
- **National** – the Scout Association of the United Kingdom organises national events and runs activity centres.
- **Global** – a world organisation promoting world friendship and peace. There are a number of international events where Scouts from different countries meet and learn from each other.

The year 2007 marked 100 years of Scouting. From just a handful of Scouts in 1907, membership has grown to over 28 million worldwide – girls and boys. There are more than 400,000 in the United Kingdom alone. A Jamboree was held in Chelmsford to mark the 100th birthday. Scouts from all over the world came and shared their different cultures, traditions and religions through their common interest in Scouting. The Jamboree also focused on climate change and recycling. Nearly 95 per cent of people who voted on the Jamboree website believed that Scouting contributed to world peace.

Scouts get involved

'Last year there was a group of Scouts in Romania who were about to set off for a regional camp. They heard about the terrible flooding that was going on in a different part of the country and decided to go there instead. They used the money, food and shelter that were supposed to be for the camp and gave it all to the people who had lost their homes. They ended up staying for two weeks, doing whatever they could.'
Ramu, Romania

(from Scout Association official website: www.scouts.org.uk)

2.2 Identities

Belonging to different communities and cultures is part of what gives people their sense of identity. It is different for every person, because some things are more important to them than others.

Look at the following influences on *cultural identity* and decide which ones are important for you.

Culture means those things that we learn from our upbringing and the people around us. It includes traditions, religious beliefs, the things we hold dear (values), food and clothes. These influence our lives and behaviour. Some of these influences we pass on to our own children.

Religion

GUTEN TAG Ahoj
Hello! Salut
नमस्ते Hej
Привет Bennos días
DoBAR DAN

Language

Family

Food

Place of birth

Education

Where you live

Symbols

Scales of Justice

Clothing

Customs and traditions

Music

Interests and hobbies

Job

Friends

Sports and teams

Activity

1 Think about examples of each of those influences that are important to you, and collect magazine pictures or draw them to make a collage of your own different identities. Look at the examples produced by some other Year 7 pupils on pages 36–7.

2 Pin the collages up on the wall and go round looking at everybody's. Talk in small groups about the different identities in the class.

- How are people different?
- What influences do people share?
- How important is your cultural identity to you?

Emma-Louise
age: 11
¼ Sri Lankan
healthy food
English
CHRISTIANITY
r&b music
trendy clothes

my IDENTITY
Born in Welwyn
Live in Hatfield
Not Religous
but have been baptised
Normal wear: Lastest fashions
Lanwage English
English
British Isles
Reb music Singers from America & England
Traditional English Roast Dinner

Different identities

Laura

My name is Laura. I am 13 years old. I live with my mum and dad and younger brother in Stevenage. We have lived in this area a long time. My dad's side of the family comes from Barnet and Watford, my mum's from London. My grandparents were born in England and I see myself as English.

I like Indian and Italian food, especially lasagne. But my favourite food is a full English breakfast – sausages, egg, bacon, the lot – and I always look forward to a Sunday roast.

I'm into dance and drama. I enjoy singing and dancing. I go to a theatre group twice a week and we rehearse and put on musicals and socialise. It is a little community. I like keeping fit and I play netball and athletics at school. I also enjoy skateboarding locally and surfing. Every year we go on holiday to Cornwall, which I really love, and I go surfing. But I would not identify myself as being a surfer or a skateboarder.

Music is important to me. Rock and Indie are my favourite music. Music has an influence on what I wear. I like Indie musicians' clothes. I dress casually, nothing fancy. Generally I am laid back although I like to do what I want to do. My family is important. We celebrate festivals and birthdays and things like that. Christmas is big.

Honesty is a big thing with me; I need to be able to trust people. I like someone who is confident. I hate racists. If people come to this country they deserve to be treated fairly. But I think they should accept the way we live and not try to change things. Polish people have a hard time around here with people passing comments about them which annoys me. There is also prejudice towards Africans and Indians.

Activity

1 Working in pairs, read all three case studies and then answer the question: What does each person see as the main features that make up their identity?

2 Add to the case studies by interviewing each other and writing up the case studies in the same style.

3 How do different cultures influence your local community? Use the illustration on page 41 to help you think about this.

Varun

My name is Varun. I live with my mum and dad and two brothers. We have lots of relatives in the area around Slough where we live. My grandparents came here from the Punjab in India. I've got quite a few cousins living in India.

I see myself as Indian Punjabi who is British. A big factor in why I think of myself as Indian is my Hindu religion. It plays a huge part in my life and in my family's life. We have a small temple upstairs at home and, when there are festivals, like Diwali, we go there and chant before going to the main temple in Slough. The festivals bring together all Indian people in community and are very important. My whole family meets up at them. Religion is in my daily life, particularly in the way we treat other people. Our religion teaches us to have respect for all animals and people whatever their nature and personality.

I don't eat any flesh or fish, I am totally vegetarian. My favourite Indian food is Palakpaneer which is spinach with a type of Indian cheese. But I also like crisps and cookies. My clothes are mostly normal, T-shirts and so on but on special occasions I dress up in Indian clothes.

My main interest is being part of a theatre group. We are putting on High School Musical at the moment. We learn dance routines, singing and acting. I like the group of people I meet there. It is very mixed but everybody gets on with each other. I also like sports. I watch football and I am a Manchester United supporter. I play basketball and cricket. I support the Indian cricket team and follow the news about the players. I started Indian drumming when I was small and now I play drums but in a Western style. I like R&B but my favourite music is Bangra and my favourite group is Punjabi MC.

Language is important to me. When I speak to my grandparents and sometimes my parents I'll speak in Hindi or Punjab which is the language they speak in the villages. It helps me when I visit India to see my relatives. We go for events like weddings or Mundan, the ceremony of the first hair cut when a relative is two years old. I really like India because it's natural and peaceful, especially in the mountains near Nepal. Cities like Delhi are very modern and exciting.

We do have some problems with racism in this area – name calling and so on. One of my friends was beaten up and injured, for no reason. The older students at the school try to find out what's going on and sort it out, check out areas near the school to make sure there's no trouble. We are all concerned about what happens to each other and will stand up and support each other.

Taylania

My name is Taylania. I am 13 years old. I live with my mum, my dad and my brother here in Hatfield. We have lived in this area for four years and before that we lived in North London. I was born in England. My grandparents came from Jamaica and Trinidad & Tobago, although one of my grandmothers was born in England.

I see myself as English and Jamaican. I eat English and Jamaican food. My favourite English food is fish and chips, my favourite Jamaican food is lamb curry. I like being English and Jamaican. I support Arsenal for football, England for cricket and Jamaica in athletics. I have visited Jamaica to see my aunts and uncles. It was really nice and different, quiet, lovely scenery, sandy beeches and blue sea. We had a house with a patio and chickens running around. I often go to help my nan with her washing and ironing and she tells me what it was like living in Jamaica. I get a picture of it in my head. I love the colours of the Jamaican flag. My dad's got one. My dad sometimes speaks in Jamaican patois and I understand it but I don't use it myself with my friends.

I have a lot of interests. I like designing my own clothes, I look at the things around me for ideas but I also like Caribbean colours which are bright and random. I love drawing; I sit with my granddad and do landscapes. I help out at a football club for ages 3–10 on Saturdays. I'm into R&B, reggae – my dad plays it – it's funky and gets you dancing. I like some pop and rock too.

My family is really important to me. We always have a big get together at birthdays. We cook up a big curry, my dad plays the music, all my aunts and uncles come. On Saturdays the whole family sits down to watch a movie with popcorn and drinks. It's important to have fun. I also want to do well at school so everyone's happy with me.

I like to stand up and say what I feel. I'm not scared and won't sit back like lots of people. I had some problems with racism in the first school I came to in this area, not this school – name calling about my colour. I don't pay much attention to little things but I don't like it if it becomes more serious.

2.3 Living together in communities

Communities do not always live happily together. Sometimes people judge each other by things like age, ethnic group, religion, wealth, class. They don't get to know each other, so they don't trust each other.

Let's look at **age**. What sorts of things do young people say about old people? What sorts of things do old people say about young people? Why do they say these things?

hoodies

binge drinkers

yobs

crinkly

moaner

crone

Activity

1 Work in pairs and write two lists:

Young people say old people are …	Old people say young people are …

2 Discuss why old and young people hold these sorts of views about each other in this country.

3 Now swap your list with another pair's list. Choose three statements from each and argue against them. In your pair, one of you will argue for old people and one for young people.

Research
You could each interview two older people and two young people to find out about their views about each other. Then you could put together a class survey.

Oldthorpe

Oldthorpe has grown a lot in the last fifteen years. New houses have been built around its edges and many new families have moved in. There are also many older retired people who used to work in the now closed car manufacturing plants.

Some of the older people are worried about the way things are going. They say they are fearful of the groups of teenagers who hang around the shopping centre. The young complain that there is nothing to do in Oldthorpe and that people pick on them when they gather to talk to their friends.

Proposals

Several proposals have been put to the local council to try to solve the problem. They include:

- opening more youth centres in the town
- opening more day care and activity centres for the elderly
- making some areas of the town (parts of parks) for old people only and other areas purely for young people (recreation areas)
- running regular events (festivals, carnivals) when old and young can mix and get to know each other
- appointing more Community Support Officers to help the security staff control the youth
- banning young people in groups of more than three from entering the shopping centre
- inviting older people to talk to the young people at school, and to work with them on projects to improve the town.

The local council is asking everyone for help and advice. A number of groups have been approached for their views.

Activity

Take on the roles of different people involved in trying to resolve this situation. Instructions and roles can be found on pages 44–5.

Instructions

1 Divide the class up into groups of 4–6 to play the following roles:
   - older residents
   - young people
   - local councillors
   - police
   - shopping centre manager and staff.

2 In your role groups, e.g. the group representing older residents, spend about 20–30 minutes discussing the proposals. Decide which you think are the best ones (or suggest what you think would be best) from the point of view of this group of people. Then choose two people from your group to put forward your ideas. You must be able to explain why you think these are the best proposals and also suggest ways to resolve the problem.

3 Hold a meeting to discuss your ideas. Elect a chairperson to control the meeting. He or she will call upon two representatives from each group to outline their ideas. The audience will be allowed to ask each group two questions. The chairperson chooses the questioners from hands raised.

4 After the group presentations, hold a general discussion, in which anybody else can add what they think. Remember that you are still in role. Again, the chairperson will select who speaks from hands raised. Once the discussion has come to an end, everyone should vote on the best idea(s).

5 Come out of role and discuss the following questions as a class:
   - Which ideas were most popular, and why?
   - Which ideas were least popular, and why?
   - Why do the young and old find it so difficult to understand each other?
   - What is the situation like in your own town or local area? What could make things better?

Roles

Older residents

You have lived and worked in Oldthorpe all your lives. It used to be a safe place – people knew each other, because most of them worked in the big car plants. Some worked on the production lines and others worked in the offices. You are not happy with the way things are now. New families have come to your town to live in the modern estates that have been built on the outskirts. They often travel into the neighbouring town to work, so people don't know each other as well as they used to. The children from these families seem out of order and unruly. There has been some vandalism, and one of your friends was insulted and threatened. The children gather in large groups in the shopping centre, so you tend not to go there any more.

What do you think could make the situation better?

Young people

Some of you were born in Oldthorpe and some came to live here when you were babies. It's your town. You have grown up here and go to school here. This is where your friends are. There is very little to do. You are too young to go into pubs, and there is very little else to amuse young people. Your parents worry about you going off into the surrounding countryside. You are always being moved on from the shopping centre, and you are accused of scaring off older people, so occasionally the police have been called.

What do you think could make the situation better?

Local councillors

You are elected members of the local council and it is your job to make sure Oldthorpe is a safe, clean and happy place for people to live. You know there's a problem at the shopping centre, where groups of young people hang around and often get moved on by the security staff. The police are sometimes called when there is trouble. You could fund some proposals to improve the situation. It seems that the older residents are frightened of the youth, and the youth feel picked on.

What do you think could make the situation better?

The police

You are senior police officers in Oldthorpe and, if something is not done about the relationship between the old and young, you can see real trouble looming in the town. Older people feel that the young have taken over the shopping centre and other parts of the town, and they are frightened to walk the streets. Your officers sometimes get called when there is trouble, but you don't want to make things worse by arresting anyone. This could create a great deal of hostility. The Community Support Officers sometimes patrol the shopping centre, but you do not think that the problem is really one that can be solved by the police.

What do you think could make the situation better?

Shopping centre manager and staff

You are responsible for the running of the Oldthorpe shopping centre and for the safety of all customers. There are seats and coffee bars in the centre that have been attracting groups of young people. They are noisy, but they seem pretty harmless. They spend some money in the music shops, clothes shops and cafés, so some of the shopkeepers don't mind them being there. However, you get many complaints from other customers because they are scared of the youth, and some of them say they won't come to the centre any more.

What do you think could make the situation better?

What happens in your nearest town centre? Have you ever thought about how it could be made better?

Activity

Working in pairs, study the picture carefully:

1 a) Find three things about this town centre that would make people like it.
  b) Find five things that would make people not like it.
2 Compare your list with the list of another pair. Do you agree about the good and bad points?
3 Which of these are similar to your nearest town centre?

Developing your research skills

Activity

1 Carry out a survey to find out what people think about your local town centre. If you do not live near a town, you could survey your village or local high street and shops. Use copies of the form opposite to collect people's opinions. You can ask other pupils, your family and friends, local shoppers and shopkeepers, the police and other people who provide services. Make sure you get opinions from people of different ages, gender and backgrounds (e.g. jobs, race, religion, etc.). If everyone in the class tries to interview about four people, you will have at least 100 responses.

Disused and run down shops

Pedestrianised shopping

2 Make charts on the computer to show the numbers of people saying what they liked and did not like about the area. Describe the things people thought were best and worst. Discuss what people thought about improvements.

3 Write a short report covering all your findings. Put forward your views about what is good and bad about the area, and what you would like to see improved.

4 Make this into a presentation that can be made to the class or an outside audience.

To illustrate what your survey has discovered, take some photographs with a digital camera to show the good and bad points about your nearest town centre.

Traffic in town centre

5 Invite a member of the local council to come into your school and discuss your report. Find out what the local council is doing about the things that need improving.
OR
Write a letter to your local councillor setting out your views and asking them to respond to your ideas.

SURVEY ON _____ CENTRE: [insert name of town]

Would you mind helping us find out what people in this area think of _____?

We are carrying out some research into people's views on the good and bad points of our local centre, and would be grateful for a few moments of your time.

1 Do you live in this area? 2 Do you work in the area? 3 Are you a visitor to the area?	Yes/No Yes/No Yes/No	
4 Which of the following do you like about the town?	Cleanliness Attractive buildings Car parking Shops Restaurants and bars Parks Safety Entertainment facilities Transport Facilities for all ages Friendliness of local people Other: [say what] _____	☐ [tick] ☐ ☐ ☐ ☐ ☐ ☐ ☐ ☐ ☐ ☐ ☐
5 Which of the following do you *not* like about the town?	Litter and graffiti Buildings Types of shops Lack of parks and green areas Restaurants and bars Feels unsafe No parking Busy roads Infrequent transport Lack of facilities for all ages Unfriendliness of local people Other: [say what] _____	☐ [tick] ☐ ☐ ☐ ☑ ☐ ☐ ☐ ☐ ☐ ☐

6 Which is the *best* thing about the town?

7 Which is the *worst* thing about the town?

8 What needs to be done to make the town better?

Thank you very much for your time.

People on television or in newspapers often say that schools should turn their pupils into good citizens. The trouble is that they don't always agree about what a 'good citizen' is. In this exercise you are going to discuss what you think this phrase means, and think about the difference between being a *good* citizen and being an *active* citizen.

1 Working in twos or threes, look at all the statements on these two pages and decide which ones make a person a **GOOD** citizen. Add two statements of your own.
2 Choose the top five statements – the ones that are most important if a person is a good citizen.
3 Now look again at all of the statements. Which ones make a person an **ACTIVE** citizen? (Some of these might be the same as for the good citizen.) Add two statements of your own.
4 Choose the top five statements – the ones that are most important if a person is an active citizen.
5 As a whole class, discuss:

   • which statements refer to being a good citizen
   • which statements refer to being an active citizen
   • whether any statements apply to being a good *and* an active citizen
   • the difference between being a good and an active citizen.

A GOOD citizen?
Or an ACTIVE citizen?

A votes in elections to choose who should run the country

B never drops litter on the streets

C takes part in local campaigns, e.g. to oppose a new building or demand a pedestrian crossing

D works for a local charity

E reports neighbours to the local authority if they are noisy

F never has parties, in case the noise disturbs the neighbours

G tells people off for dropping litter or letting their dogs foul the street

H obeys all laws and rules at all times

I stays out late at night having a good time with friends

J takes newspapers and bottles to the recycling centre

K watches the neighbours very closely to make sure they are not up to mischief

L has strong religious beliefs and worships regularly

M takes part in election campaigns by distributing leaflets for a political party

N takes part in protests over important issues (e.g. where a road is being built through a beauty spot), even if this means breaking the law

O does not write graffiti on walls

P reports vandals to the police

Q takes part in a Neighbourhood Watch group to prevent crime

R is pleasant to people if they ask for help (e.g. giving directions)

S takes books back to the library on time

T votes in elections to choose who should run the local council

U helps elderly neighbours and pops round to check they are OK

V does not talk loudly on a mobile phone in a public place

W does not put their feet on the seats of buses and trains

X takes an interest in current affairs and watches the news

Y writes letters to MPs (Members of Parliament) or the local council about things that seem wrong

Some people say ...
A 'good citizen' is someone who is easy to get on with and to live near, because he or she obeys the rules, helps others, and is responsible and considerate.

Some people say ...
An 'active citizen' is also responsible, but wants to change things for the better. He or she is prepared to point out things that are not so good, to argue and take actions that will persuade other people that change is necessary.

As an active citizen you can help to make your community a better place to live. You can try to influence the decisions of the local council, who are responsible for looking after your local area. What else can you do to have your say on what's going on in your neighbourhood?

Activity

1 The issues below might occur in any local area. Working in pairs, look at the 'What could you do?' box opposite and decide which course of action you think is appropriate in each case. Some issues are more serious than others, so you need to find an appropriate solution. Use your own ideas as well when deciding what could be done.

2 As a whole class, compare the decisions you reached. Discuss why you chose one course of action rather than another.

A Your rubbish is not being collected regularly.

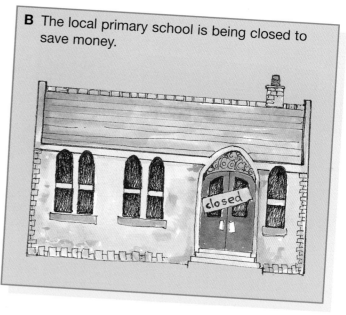

B The local primary school is being closed to save money.

C Some neighbours in your area are very noisy. One household down the road often plays music until 3a.m.

D A new supermarket is being built in the neighbourhood. Most local people do not want another supermarket. You want a leisure centre or an ice rink.

E The council has agreed to allow a building developer to remove a large number of ancient trees. They were part of the common land near where you live, which is a site of great natural beauty, housing rare butterflies.

F A particular place where people cross the road has been the scene of a number of accidents. (There is nowhere else on the road to cross.) You have begged the council to put in a proper pelican crossing, but nothing has been done yet. After the latest accident, in which a girl broke her leg, you agree with other local people that something has to be done.

What could you do?

This list shows some of the things you could do to tackle these issues.

1 Ring up the council and talk to the official responsible.
2 Write a letter of complaint to the council.
3 Go to see your local councillor. They usually hold regular 'surgeries' to listen to the complaints and problems of the people in their area.
4 Draw up a petition to send to the council.
5 If the council does not respond, write to the local newspaper.
6 Organise a local demonstration or march in connection with the issue. Invite the local newspaper along, and invite local councillors to join you.
7 Take part in peaceful, but disruptive, behaviour, e.g. sitting down in the road, occupying houses or areas of countryside.

Being an active citizen

When things in our communities are not right, it's easy to moan and complain. But perhaps something could be done. When people work together, they can often help to make changes happen.

Activity

Work in small groups and choose one of the issues below.
  OR
Choose an issue in your school or neighbourhood that concerns you – something you would like to change or improve. Think carefully about this as you could actually take real action to change things.

Decide what action needs to be taken to improve things, and what you could do to make it happen. Complete the action plan opposite.

School dinners are unhealthy, small and expensive.

The local park/recreation ground is dirty and dangerous, with no play area and equipment for young children.

The youth club is only open on Tuesday and Thursday evenings.

Bullying is common in the school playground.

The buses are often full and the drivers won't let schoolchildren on.

Action plan

	Action	Comments
IDENTIFY THE ISSUE What is wrong or needs changing?		

	Action	Comments
CARRY OUT RESEARCH What information do we need? Where shall we look for information? How will we find out what other people think about this issue? How could things be improved?		
PLAN AND CARRY OUT ACTION What different kinds of action could we take? Who can help us? Who will we work with? What action shall we definitely take?		

REFLECT ON THE ACTION
(Only fill out this section if you have carried out an action)

What worked well?

What didn't work well?

What should we have done differently?

Was the action successful?

Feeling that you belong to a community is important, but so is how the area looks, what it is like to live there now, and what it will be like in the future. One of the biggest problems in any area is waste. We don't want smelly rubbish and old sofas lying around the streets. But getting rid of waste is increasingly tricky, and some difficult decisions have to be made about how we do it. Individual citizens have a responsibility for this, as well as councils and businesses.

Over 70 per cent of the waste we produce locally is sent to landfill, which means it is buried in the ground. Around 10 per cent is incinerated (that is, it is burned). Both of these have a bad effect on the environment. Landfill creates gases and can pollute water sources, while incineration produces harmful gases and ash. In addition, we are running out of landfill sites, and nobody wants to live next to a landfill site or an incinerator! On top of this, it's a huge waste of the world's resources such as wood, metals and oil, which are decreasing. Some people argue that, after climate change, waste is humankind's biggest problem.

So, what can we do about it?
We can:

Wacky waste facts

Every year:

> The UK produces more than 434 million tonnes of waste every year, which is enough to fill the Royal Albert Hall in London in less than two hours.
> We throw away from our homes rubbish the same weight as 3.5 million double-decker buses.
> Each person in the UK throws away an average of seven times their body weight in rubbish.
> Every family disposes of an average of 330 glass bottles and jars.
> Supermarkets give away 17.5 million plastic bags.
> We use up a forest the size of Wales to provide us with paper.

(*from www.wasteonline.com*)

Reduce – cut down the amount of waste we produce

Reuse – use some things again

Recycle – collect and turn resources back into things that we can use

Reducing and re-using

Although many local councils are encouraging people to recycle waste, we can also make sure that we produce less waste in the first place. We can do this by reducing what we buy and re-using what we have. For example, waste food is being recycled as fertilizer by many local councils. But there would be less waste if people bought less food (reduced it) and used up left-overs (re-used it).

Products

- Clothes
- Toys
- Shoes
- Plastic bags
- Glass bottles
- Books

- China
- Computers
- Mobile phones
- Packaging
- Furniture

Ways of reducing waste or re-using products

Charity shop

Car boot sale

Cloth shopping bag

Refill facility

Milkman

Council van collecting second hand furniture

Veg being sold in paper bag

Home made jam and pickles

Charity leaflet

The Government Waste and Resources Action Programme (WRAP), says we throw away nearly 7 million tons of food each year – enough to fill Wembley Stadium eight times. For every three bags of shopping brought home, one ends up in landfill.

Activity

Look at the pictures showing ways we can reduce waste and re-use products. Then decide how we can use these (and any other ways you can think of) in regard to the products on the list.

Activity

1 Find out more by looking at websites to do with reducing and re-using waste. Start with www.recyclezone.org.uk, www.wasteonline.org.uk and www.recyclenow.com
2 Carry out a survey among your friends and family to see how many of them use these methods of reducing waste.

Recycling

All councils now collect some items from the doorstep and provide recycling bins or bags. They want to recycle as much waste as possible, as they have to pay high prices to send rubbish to landfill sites. But only a small percentage of our rubbish is recycled, and many people still can't be bothered to help. There has been some discussion about how people could be persuaded to recycle more of their waste.

Activity

Look at the ways suggested below to encourage people to recycle more. Working in groups of three or four, answer these questions:

1 What are the advantages and disadvantages of the different schemes?
2 Which of them do you think would work best, and why?
3 Which ones would not work?
4 How would you persuade people to recycle more?

Rewards for households who recycle – for example, £50 a year cashback – while non-recyclers pay more (say, £50 extra).

Charge people for non-recycled rubbish by weight. This would be done by having a chip in the dustbin which would keep a record of the weight. The charge could be 50p per kilo. Recycled items would be collected free.

Prize draws (up to £1000) for participating in kerbside collection schemes.

Make households who don't recycle pay fines or more Council Tax. Their rubbish would be inspected to see if they are recycling.

Collect non-recyclable rubbish once a fortnight instead of once a week, as this would encourage people to put out less. Collect recycled goods more often.

Campaigning

The UK is one of the worst countries in Europe for reducing and recycling waste. Campaigners are trying to persuade consumers and businesses to reduce the waste they produce. Two big offenders are:

- supermarkets, who create an enormous amount of packaging waste, and hand out millions of free plastic bags
- companies who hand out free newspapers, which create a mountain of paper and litter.

Here are some comments from a BBC website:

I've always said that supermarkets use far too much packaging. Just look at this roast chicken – it's in a tray, which is in a bag, which is then bagged in plastic. They say it's for hygiene reasons, but it wasn't needed in my day. Overpackaged fruit and veg rile me, too!

In Switzerland plastic bottles for water and soft drinks have a deposit on them and can be returned for reuse, as can beer bottles and some wine bottles. When visiting my Swiss girlfriend in Zurich, she demonstrated a simple and effective way of encouraging supermarkets to deal with the packaging problem – take it off the product and leave it in the supermarket.

I live in Tokyo, where under strict laws we have to separate out rubbish each week. Mondays are plastic items, Wednesdays and Saturdays are everyday rubbish and food scraps, and Thursdays are cans, bottles, plastic bottles and Polystyrene and even milk cartons. It was a pain at first, but after a few weeks it became a habit.

Activity

Working in groups, plan a campaign to encourage people to reduce, reuse or recycle materials. Produce a leaflet or poster to promote your campaign. Here are some ideas, although you can use one of your own. You will find lots of information on the internet about these topics.

1 Persuade supermarkets to reduce their packaging and plastic bags. Methods you could use: letters, leaflets, petition, demonstrations.
2 Persuade people to reuse materials. Show people how they could do this, and find out what sorts of things can be reused. Look at Freecycle on www.freecycle.org.
3 Persuade people of the benefits to them of recycling, and why it is important for the environment. Use examples from other countries. Look at your local council website to see what they do in your neighbourhood.

Lots of different groups of people live in towns, boroughs and villages. They have different interests, backgrounds, traditions and beliefs, but they all need to know what is happening in their area, and be kept up-to-date with information and with stories that affect them.

Many communities now have their own websites. The sites include information about the community, its history and facilities, its local businesses and tourist attractions. Stories of local interest are featured and the sites sometimes have an 'Add news' facility and a message board, so that anyone can get a story published or comment on items posted. There is usually a 'moderator' who looks at contributions to make sure that stories posted are not offensive.

You can search through the internet to find examples – just type 'community websites' into a search engine. Websites can make people feel part of their community, so long as everyone's stories and interests are represented. Have a look at some real ones and decide which ones are the most successful at doing this.

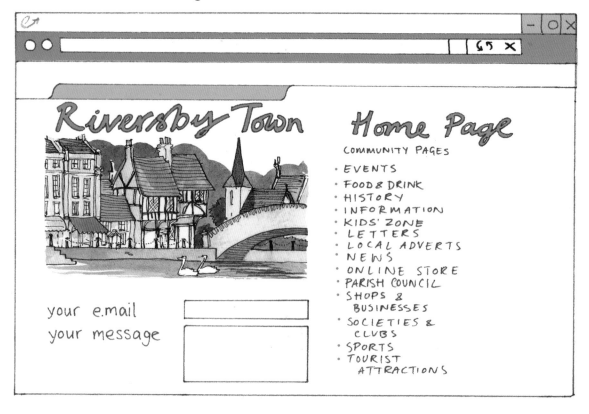

Make your own community webpage

Activity

Work in large groups of up to ten. Design a webpage about your local community. Or you could use a community website builder, such as www.communitykit.co.uk.

You already know a lot about your local community, but you will need to find out much more about information and local issues. Collect local newspapers and look at websites which have information about what is going on in your area. Ask people who live in the area what some of the important issues are. Make sure that everyone is able to have their say on the story, so include a message board.

1 Discuss which local issues might make good stories or items. These might include items about local schools, crime, parks, graffiti, recycling, facilities for old people, planning applications, animals – you decide. You can also include items about your school – sports results or open evenings. Be sure that you cover items that include lots of different groups in the community.

2 Decide who will take on the three main jobs: journalists, editors and designers. Give out the jobs to each group.

The journalists
- Your job is to find the stories and items for the webpage. Write about 50 to 100 words on each.
- Some items will just give information about your community, some will cover the issue mentioned above.
- Give each story/item a title.
- Add photos if you can find them, with captions.

The editors
- Your job is to collect the stories and decide which ones you are going to use.
- Check the writing, correct any mistakes, and make sure the stories read well.
- Work out how the items all fit together on the page.
- You can also help the journalists research the items/stories.
- Encourage readers to respond to the stories by including links to the message board.

The designers
- Your job is to set up and design the webpage.
- Make sure it can be easily used and looks attractive to users.
- Include a message board.
- Follow the guidance of the editors on entering the items and pictures.
- You can also help the journalists research the items/stories.

When you have finished your webpage, ask some members of the local community to look at it, to give some idea of what people would think of it if it went live.

Reflection

How well do you think you're doing?
Think back over the work you've done in Section 2.

Skills

- Draw a chart like the one below, and give yourself a grade from 1 to 5, where 1 is the lowest and 5 is the highest.
- Give evidence for your score and say how you could improve your skills.

How well can you … ?	1	2	3	4	5	Evidence for your score?	How can you improve?
express your opinions							
see things from another person's point of view							
interview people to collect information in a survey							
put together the results of a survey							
present your ideas to an audience							
plan a campaign of action							

Understanding

- Complete the following sentences:
  'An active citizen is …'
  'Active citizens can change their communities by …'
- Why are the following important in people's 'identities'?

- Talk to another pupil and discuss what you think was the most important thing you learned in this section.

Section 3

Being a global citizen

How are you connected to other countries?

What ideas do you have about other countries?

How are your ideas shaped by images in the media?

Can you do anything to make the world a fairer place?

Should you help people in other countries, and what can you do?

We say 'the world is shrinking' because it is so easy to communicate with people instantly using telephones and the internet, wherever they are in the world. People travel to different countries for holidays, on business, to visit relatives, to work and to live. We are connected to other countries by trade, and most of the goods we buy in shops are made abroad. We also have responsibilities to other countries when there are natural disasters, such as floods and volcanoes, or man-made disasters like wars, which cause great suffering and distress. What happens in one part of the world affects other parts. We are all becoming global citizens.

Assessing your progress
In this section you will:

- express and explain views that may not be your own
- speak up for other people
- listen to other people's views
- research using the internet
- develop your understanding of global issues.

KEY WORDS

global interdependence

fair trade

charities

We all have our own ideas about what other countries are like. Many of us have friends and relatives who have lived in or were born in other countries. Some of us were born abroad ourselves. Lots of people from this country go on holidays to places in different parts of the world.

Activity

You need a blank world map and an atlas. Work in groups of four or five.

1 As a group, list all the countries where someone in the group has relatives living. Mark these countries on the map with a red cross.
2 Now list all the countries that you have visited – be it on holiday or to visit relatives – or where you have lived. Identify these countries with a blue cross.
3 How many countries have you marked? List them all. Write them all up on a large sheet of paper. When all groups have done this, see how many countries appear on the list.
4 You could put a huge map of the world on the wall and plot the connections for the entire class.

Research

If your school has links with other countries, ask these contacts what image they have of people in the UK. You could conduct an online survey of people's customs and habits, e.g. food and eating habits, clothes, hobbies, sports, how they spend their leisure time and so on. Devise your own questions for this.

Rich and poor

When people talk about the world as a whole, they like to divide it into 'rich' countries and 'poor' countries. Rich countries are likely to be in Europe, North America, Australia and parts of Asia, while chances are that the poor countries are in Africa, Asia and Latin America. However, this division is too simple, because not everybody in a rich country is rich, and not every person in a poor country is poor. Richer countries have all sorts of problems, such as pollution, crime, homelessness and unemployment. The problem is that, when we hear about people in poorer countries, it is usually when they have been affected by some sort of disaster. This gives the impression that nothing else happens in these countries.

People also use other names to describe the division between countries:

Rich	Poor
Developed	Developing or Underdeveloped
First World	Third World or Majority World
North	South
More Economically Developed Country (MEDC)	Less Economically Developed Country (LEDC)

DISCUSS

1 Brainstorm the images you have of the following countries and the people who live there: Italy, Saudi Arabia, the United States, Ethiopia, India and China.

2 Has anyone in the class been to any of these countries? If so, do they agree with the images?

3 Where do we get our images of other countries from?

Images of developing countries

What images do you have of other countries referred to as Third World or developing countries?

On these two pages, you can see two collections of images: Collection A and Collection B.

Collection A

Collection B

Activity

1 Look at Collection A. What ideas about the people from these countries do these pictures give you?

2 Look at Collection B.

  a) What ideas about the people do these pictures suggest?

  b) How are they different from the pictures in Collection A?

3 Which collection is closer to the view you had formed of developing countries?

4 Why do you think we see so many of the type of images in Collection A in our media and very few of Collection B?

5 How does this affect our views of the people who live in developing countries?

Although you may not realise it, you are connected to other parts of the world in many different ways. You just have to look at the food in your cupboard and see where the ingredients come from, or at your clothes and other things you own, to see where they were made. There are all sorts of links that connect us to the cultures and people of other countries.

Our connections with the world

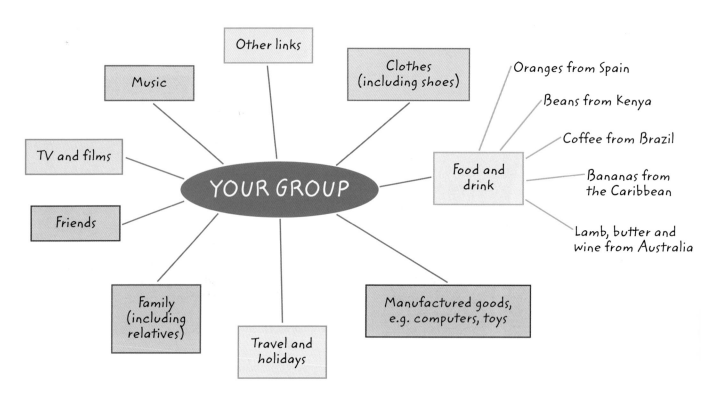

Interdependence – the good and the bad

Countries depend on each other for things they need – they are interdependent. For instance, in the UK we need food, goods and energy from other countries, and many other things besides. This allows us to enjoy a more varied and comfortable lifestyle. But there can also be disadvantages to these connections. While some people gain, others can lose.

Activity

Make a copy of the grid below, which lists some of our main connections with other countries. Then look at the statements below the grid, which describe some of the advantages and disadvantages of these links. Match each statement with one of the topics by putting its letter in the appropriate column.

Global connection through …	Advantage	Disadvantage	One other advantage/ disadvantage
Food			
Manufactured goods			
Holidays and tourism			
Clothes and shoes			
Raw materials such as wood and metals			

A Travelling by plane is much cheaper than it used to be, so you can go to far-off places for your holidays and see how people live.

B Imported clothes are often made by people who work long hours for little pay, often in very unpleasant conditions.

C Supermarkets offer foods and ingredients from all over the world, so we can get fruit, like apples, all year round.

D Big hotels can ruin beaches and the natural environment.

E We can buy cheap, fashionable clothes and replace them as soon as they go out of fashion.

F The world's forests are being cut down and this damages the world's climate, because trees give us oxygen.

G The factories that make manufactured goods cause environmental damage.

H We need imported wood for building houses and making paper.

I Some food travels huge distances, called 'food miles' – for example, bringing beans from Kenya by aeroplane – which contributes to climate change.

J We get goods like computers, hi-fis, MP3 players and vacuum cleaners cheaply, because they are made in places where wages are low.

DISCUSS

Can you suggest any ways of overcoming some of these disadvantages?

3.3 Hard labour!

We like to buy goods like trainers, T-shirts and footballs as cheaply as we can. It means we have more money to spend on other things. But sometimes these goods have been made by people, including children, who work very long hours for very low wages, and usually in terrible conditions.

Activity

Read the extract from the United Nations Convention on the Rights of the Child on page 72 and the case studies on these pages. As you read them:

a) decide which rights are being denied to the children in the case studies

b) list the ways that their lives are affected by their work.

Facts and figures

It is difficult to be accurate, but it is estimated that around the world more than 200 million children aged from five to fourteen work as child labourers. The highest numbers are in Asia and sub-Saharan Africa, but there are also many in richer industrialised countries. In the USA, thousands of Mexican-American children help harvest crops. There are also child workers in the UK.

Case study 1

The ball you play football with might well come from India. Sonia is eleven years old and stitches soccer balls. She lives in a village in India's Punjab. She is blind – she lost her sight at the age of seven – but she has learned to stitch soccer balls by touch alone. Her aunt passes her the panels to sew. Since Sonia's mother fell seriously ill, she is one of the main breadwinners for the family.

'There's no fun in it, but I have no choice,' says Sonia, who earns seven rupees a day – not even enough to buy a litre of milk.

(Adapted from the *New Internationalist*)

Case study 2

Vinod is aged ten and lives in Dariyen village, in the Indian state of Uttar Pradesh. He worked for two years for a carpet weaver. Manufacturers like to employ children because they are cheap, and they say the children have small hands and nimble fingers. Long hours of work lead to illness, and sitting in cramped positions can lead to malformed bones. Meanwhile, these child labourers miss out on their education and have fewer chances of a good job later on.

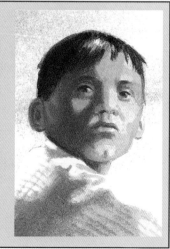

   Vinod remembers those horrifying days with deep pain. 'I used to work twelve to fourteen hours a day on the loom. I was not paid a single penny for a year. A week after joining, I was hung upside down for a minor fault. If I got injuries from using a sharp knife to turn the carpet knots, I was denied medical care. Instead, my employer used to fill the wound with matchstick powder and burn it. My flesh and skin used to burn.'

Case study 3

Elias and Ramiro Jankho are brothers who work in the Santa Rosa mine in Bolivia, digging for silver, lead and zinc. Ramiro, who is twelve years old, pushes a wheelbarrow of rough metal ore through the dark passageways of the mine. His ten-year-old brother, Elias, helps him heave it up to the surface in a bucket attached to a rope. There is no safety system in the mine. Miners hack ore from the rock with hammer and chisel, much as they did 400 years ago. Many of them become ill from the dust and grit in the mine. The boys are not paid, as they help their father earn a living – around £2.70 per day for an adult miner. Sometimes they get food and clothes. Both go to school, but not regularly.

(Adapted from case study written by Chris Holt for Cafod)

Case study 4

Chocolate is a tasty treat for most people. Not for twelve-year-old Marc, though; he has never tried it. Yet Marc lives in a country that grows half of the world's cocoa beans, the main ingredient used to make chocolate. Every day in the Ivory Coast, he and thousands of boys like him are forced into the dangerous work of harvesting the cocoa beans to supply our demand for chocolate.

Chocolate manufacturers based in the UK and other Western countries control the chocolate industry, and they choose to pay very low prices for the cocoa beans. As African cocoa farmers do not earn enough to hire adult labour, they then force children like Marc to work, paying them very little money, or often nothing at all.

Marc works for his father, Jean Kwame, on a cocoa plantation in the village of Allanbakro. 'I teach Marc to work the land. Life is very poor for us. This is how we live. We make no money.' Using dangerous equipment like cocoa machetes, Marc often suffers deep cuts to his legs that are left untreated. Both he and other young children learn to cope with flies feasting on their weeping wounds as they work long hours in the unbearable heat, cutting, sifting and stacking beans. Marc is trapped in this daily cycle, and he is also banned from seeing his mother. 'I used to go to school, but my father said there is no boy to work in the field, so then he made me work. My mother is a long way from here. I haven't seen her for ten years, since I was two years old.'

(By Mark Charman, based on the 2007 documentary *Bitter-Sweet* by Humphrey Hawksley)

The United Nations Convention on the Rights of the Child

Below are extracts from a summary of the Convention, which was written for children by UNICEF in 1989.

Article 3: Whenever an adult has anything to do with you, they should do what is best for you.

Article 12: Whenever adults make a decision which will affect you in any way, you have the right to give your opinion, and the adults to take that seriously.

Article 14: You have the right to think what you like and be whatever religion you want to be. Your parents should help you learn what is right and wrong.

Article 15: You have the right to meet, make friends and make clubs with other people, unless it interferes with the rights of others.

Article 19: No one should hurt you in any way. Adults should make sure you are protected from abuse, violence and neglect.

Article 23: If you are disabled, either mentally or physically, you have the right to special care and education to grow up in the same way as other children.

Article 24: You have the right to good health. This means you should have professional care and medicines when you are sick.

Article 27: You have the right to a good enough 'standard of living'. This means that parents have the responsibility to make sure that you have food, clothes, a place to live, etc. If parents cannot afford this, the government should help.

Article 28: You have the right to education … and [primary education] must be free.

Article 31: You have the right to play and leisure.

Article 32: You have the right to be protected from working places or conditions that are likely to damage your health or get in the way of your education. If somebody is making money out of your work, you should be paid fairly.

DISCUSS

Are there any of these rights that you think might be difficult to put into practice?

Child protection in the UK

Some of the rights contained in the Convention can be seen in measures already put in place in the UK. All the examples below are ways of protecting children:

- Education was made compulsory and also free more than 100 years ago, because some parents could not afford to send their children to school and because employers wanted cheap child workers to work in the fields or in industrial jobs.
- There is a law to stop you taking paid work before the age of 13, and you can only work for a very limited number of hours until you are older.
- Social services can take children away from their parents in the best interests of the child, especially if the child is being hurt or neglected.
- Children are not allowed to buy alcohol, cigarettes or fireworks.

DISCUSS

1 Do you agree that the measures above protect children? Why, or why not?
2 Would you like to change any of them? If so, how?
3 Would you like to introduce new measures to protect children in the UK?

What can you do about child workers?

We are global consumers – we buy goods from all over the world. If enough people get together, they can influence the companies that sell the goods in our shops. But is it anything to do with us?

Activity

Discuss the statements below with a partner. Which do you agree with, disagree with or can't decide about? What do you think should be done?

> It's simple. If the goods are made by children, then we stop buying them. We should boycott* the goods now. Then the companies will stop employing children.

> It's nothing to do with us. If the goods are cheap, buy them. We don't know what's going on in other countries.

> We should write to our MPs to make the government put pressure on the governments of the other countries to stop the use of child labour.

> It's really up to the governments of the countries where the children are used as cheap labour. If they're not worried about it, then why should we be?

> We should give the companies a year or two to stop using children and replace them with adults. If they don't, we should boycott* all their products.

> We must put pressure on the companies by having campaigns in this country, and demonstrating and protesting outside shops that sell the goods.

> Demonstrating and protesting do not achieve anything. We are powerless to influence big multinational companies.

* This means to refuse to buy or handle goods as a means of protest.

Activity

Solving problems like child labour is not always straightforward. The actions we take can have consequences that we did not intend.

1 Look at the diagram below and the working children's statements. Compare these with your answers from the previous exercise on page 73. How does this change your view about what should be done?

2 Why do you think the children are against boycotts? Why do they want to work?

do backbreaking agricultural work

become a street child

end up sifting through rubbish for anything of value

What might happen if the children lost their jobs?

family can't buy clothes or shoes

become involved in the child sex market

family goes hungry because of extra money lost

The working children's statements

The children who are worst treated will probably never have a chance to complain. But young adults and working children in different countries have started movements to try to improve their conditions of work. Here are some of the statements they have made:

- We are against the boycott of products made by children.
- We want an education system and teaching methods suited to the reality of our lives.
- We want professional training suited to our needs and capabilities.
- We want access to good health care.
- We want to be consulted on all decisions affecting us, at local, national and international level.
- We want the root causes of our situation, primarily poverty, to be tackled.
- We are against exploitation at work, but we are for work with dignity, with hours adapted so that we have time for education and leisure.

Taking action

Big companies are affected by public pressure. They do not like bad publicity about their products or the threat that consumers will not buy their goods. As a result, some companies now insist that children below a certain age do not work in their factories. Some invest in the areas where children work and contribute to their education. Some have put in place other schemes, e.g. health care and better housing. But there is a long way to go and there are still many rich companies using cheap labour in developing countries.

What the pupils of one school did

The pupils of Gallion's Primary School were horrified when they found out about the terrible conditions under which children lived and worked in the cocoa industry on the Ivory Coast. They found out that children of their age were employed in cutting and collecting the cocoa beans that are used to make chocolate. The children worked for long hours for very little money.

The British children decided to do something about it:

- Some of them stopped eating chocolate unless it was fair trade chocolate (see page 76).
- They wrote to the chocolate industry to tell them why they were upset and why the companies should help the child workers.
- They put on a play to dramatise and raise awareness of the conditions of the child workers.
- They wrote letters to politicians and managed to speak to a government minister.
- Eventually they ended up on BBC *Newsnight*, where several of the children confronted a representative of the chocolate manufacturers. They asked her some hard questions about why the companies had not done more to help the children and their families.

7p to cocoa farmers

7p tax in Ghana

17.5p tax in the UK

28p to shops

40.5p to companies making chocolate

Where the money goes from a £1 chocolate bar

DISCUSS

Now that you've read everything in this section on child labour, what do you think are the best ways of helping these children?

Activity

Design a poster or leaflet to make people aware of child labour, and suggest how we can help to improve the lives of the child labourers. You will find a lot more information on the internet. Type 'child workers' into a search engine.

One way to support poorer people in the developing world is through fair trade. Many farmers who grow products such as tea, coffee, cocoa, cotton and bananas have to sell their crop to traders who pay very little. The money they earn is often less than the cost of harvesting the crop, and they live in constant debt. They can't afford to send their children to school or improve their homes. Some who work on plantations owned by large companies are paid very low wages, live in poor housing, work in unsafe conditions and are not allowed to join trade unions.

- **Fair trade** means paying farmers in the developing world a fair and stable price for what they produce. This means that they can have more control over their lives, and improve their standard of living.
- **The FAIRTRADE Mark** is a consumer label. It guarantees that the farmers who produced the food originally were paid a fair price.
- **The Fairtrade Foundation** awards the Fairtrade Mark to products that meet agreed criteria (or standards) – in other words, products that really are fairly traded.

Activity

For products to be allowed to carry the FAIRTRADE Mark, certain conditions have to be met. You can see some of these in the table opposite. Working in small groups, decide whether the products described opposite:

- should be awarded the FAIRTRADE Mark
- should NOT be awarded the Mark
- could be awarded the Mark if certain things were improved.

You will not find all the criteria in the descriptions, but see if they meet enough to be given the Mark.

Guarantees a **better deal** for Third World Producers ®

FAIRTRADE

FAIRTRADE Mark guarantees	Yes	No	Only if …
1 The price paid for the product covers the cost of producing it			
2 Workers have decent wages, housing, and health and safety standards			
3 No child labour or forced labour is allowed			
4 An extra sum of money is paid to improve the workers' living and working conditions			
5 The environment is treated in a sustainable way*			
6 Farmers and workers can join organisations that will support them, e.g. cooperatives or trade unions			

* This means that the environment is cared for and not damaged, e.g. by destroying forests or by overusing harmful pesticides that may affect the soil, as well as the health of humans.

Tea
We run a small tea estate in northern India, producing delicious tea. The harsh environment here means we have to use chemicals on our crop. We do have protective clothing for the tea pickers, but most of them choose not to wear it because it's so hot. We cannot afford to pay our workers very much, but we will employ their families if they want them to work. Just over 30 per cent of the tea pickers' children aged 6 to 12 go to school on the estate. If a worker is absent after an accident at work, we have agreed to pay up to three days' wages. We provide housing for our workers, made of bamboo, mud and thatch. They do not have electricity or piped water. We hope to invest money to improve things in the future if we get a good price for our tea.

Brazil nuts
We are a small trading company in Peru. We buy Brazil nuts from families living in the Amazon rainforest. The men, women and children gather the wild Brazil nuts and carry them to the river. We pay them a fair price for people in this area. This is not high, but people here do not earn much. We would like to help them with their houses, but they prefer to live in their own huts in the forest. We have been thinking about setting up some schools. The nuts go by boat to the shelling factory in the nearest town. Then they are flown to Lima, sorted, graded and packed, ready for export to Europe. The European price will cover our production costs and leave a good profit.

Sugar
We are a cooperative in the Philippines. We grow and mill our own sugar. Our members receive 5 to 10 per cent more pay than other local workers. We elect a committee to make decisions about issues like health and safety. We are gradually improving our homes; all our children now go to school, and we help with the costs of schoolbooks and uniforms. We do not use harmful chemicals on our crops. We have a training programme for our farmers, and encourage the women in our community to develop their own businesses – some are raising chickens and pigs; others are making craft items to sell in the local town.

DISCUSS

1 Would you be prepared to pay a little bit more for fair trade products?
2 How would you encourage supermarkets to stock more fair trade products?

You will be familiar with appeals made by charities for money to help people in other countries, especially after disasters caused by floods, earthquakes or drought. Sometimes the affected countries are quite prosperous and charities are needed to help people get through a difficult time. However, much of the work that charities do in developing countries is concerned with longer-term projects to help the people help themselves.

Books

Wells

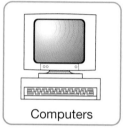
Computers

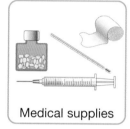
Medical supplies

Doctors

Food

Seeds

Hospitals

Tools

Blankets and clothing

Tents

Fresh water supplies

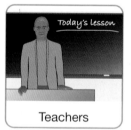
Teachers

Irrigation

Tractors

Activity

The pictures show some of the different things that charities do. Put each one into one of the categories shown in the chart.

Help in emergencies and disasters	Long-term development work to help people help themselves

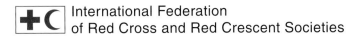 International Federation of Red Cross and Red Crescent Societies

 Oxfam

 christian aid

How Oxfam is helping

Civil wars, tribal struggles and ongoing conflicts over natural resources have left large parts of Sudan desperately poor and underdeveloped. In recent years, the western region of Darfur has seen one of the world's worst humanitarian crises. Oxfam are providing emergency support to those affected by intensifying violence in Darfur. In the north and south of the country, their work focuses on helping people to make a secure living. They provide small loans and run training schemes to help women, in particular, build a secure livelihood.

Oxfam's other work in Sudan:

- peace-building initiatives
- improving educational opportunities
- supplying clean water.

'With the money we have earned, we have been able to build ourselves proper homes, made out of concrete. We can pay our children's school fees and buy medicines when they get sick.'

How WaterAid is helping

 DISCUSS

WaterAid

Shortage of water and contaminated water are responsible for millions of deaths each year, as well as disease and illness, especially among children. Some people, often women and children, have to travel hours to get water. Water is very heavy and can damage people's necks and backs.

WaterAid aims to help all people have access to clean and safe water. Clean water and good sanitation could cut the number of deaths of children under 5 years old by as much as 50 per cent. WaterAid works with local people on projects to:

- bring safe water to villages by digging wells or laying pipes
- improve sanitation facilities to reduce the spread of diseases
- educate families in good hygiene practices.

1 These cartoons represent four different ways in which charities work with people. What are they?
2 Which of these can you identify in the Oxfam and WaterAid case studies?
3 Do you think it is important to involve the people from local communities in development projects, or should the work be done for them?

Should you help?

Most people support charities and the work they do in developing countries. But some people argue that it is not always a good idea to give lots of money to charities. People talk about 'compassion fatigue'; that is to say, we are tired of being asked to give to this and that charity. What do you think?

DISCUSS

1 Look at the statements below. Decide whether you agree or disagree with each statement.
2 Discuss the statements as a whole class. Are there any other reasons that you can think of why we should or should not help?

A We should always help people worse off than ourselves. It is morally the right thing to do.

B If we don't help people in trouble, others might not help us when we are in need.

C Other people's problems are nothing to do with me.

D How can anyone see pictures of human suffering and not help? Especially when it's children.

E Helping people in poor countries makes them dependent on aid. We should encourage them to help themselves.

F We're just pouring money down a huge drain. We spend millions and there is not much to show for it.

G The real problem is overpopulation. People in poor countries should have smaller families.

H Poor countries are poor because of the way rich people treated them in the past. We owe it to poor countries to help them.

I Money that I give to charity might end up in the pocket of someone dishonest, not helping people in need.

J We should help people in this country before giving money for other countries.

K It's a religious duty to help people wherever they live.

Developing your campaigning skills

Another important aspect of the work of charities is campaigning. It is not enough to help people in emergencies or to support them with longer-term development work. Sometimes you have to put pressure on governments, companies or individuals to change the way they are doing things. This is particularly the case where the human rights of people are involved and there is a great deal of human suffering.

You have already seen that an effective campaign can be mounted by primary school pupils (on page 75). You will also be able to find a large number of campaigns on the internet, run by various organisations. You can find some of these in the box on the right; you could look at these while doing the activity.

> **Organisations that run campaigns**
> Anti-Slavery International
> Oxfam ('Get Involved' section)
> Christian Aid
> War on Want
> Greenpeace
> World Wildlife Fund
> Friends of the Earth

Activity

Work in groups. Your task is to draw up an action plan for a campaign. Use this framework to guide you.

1 What is the **issue** you are campaigning about? You could choose one of these topics, or think up your own:

- fair trade
- child labour
- clean water
- free education.

2 What are the **aims** of your campaign?
3 Next, **who** are you going to target your campaign at?

- the government
- companies
- the public
- all of these
- somebody else

4 What **methods** are you going to use to persuade your target audience?

- posters
- leaflets
- mailshots
- newspaper articles
- local radio
- petitions
- fundraising events
- school assemblies
- badges
- other ways

When each group has planned its campaign, organise a class presentation to decide which is the best campaign for the class to adopt. You could invite some charity workers in to hear your presentations.

Each presentation should be assessed by the class, using the following scale:

	Low				High
Interesting (I enjoyed listening)	1	2	3	4	5
Informative (I learned something new)	1	2	3	4	5
Persuasive (I agree with the aims)	1	2	3	4	5

Many people like to travel abroad for their holidays. They are not just looking for the sun and beaches. They enjoy visiting other countries where the food, music, buildings, history and customs are all different from home. Tourism has become the single biggest industry on Earth. It creates enormous incomes for some countries, and many people now depend on tourism for their jobs and livelihoods.

Activity

What do tourists want from a holiday? In pairs, look at the pictures and decide the six most important things a country needs if it wants to create a successful holiday industry. List them in order of importance.

Entertainment – music venues, theatres

Restaurants and cafés

Workers (for hotels, restaurants, etc.)

Historic buildings and sites

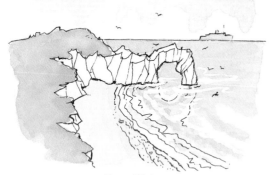
Beautiful scenery

Beaches and watersports

Transport – coaches, cars for hire, trains, taxis

Airport

Shops and markets

Foreign-language speakers (guides, etc.)

Hotels, apartments and villas

Nightclubs

Swimming pools

Bars

Museums and art galleries

How does tourism affect you?

You are likely to be affected by tourism, even if you don't go on holiday yourself. Put the following into two lists – 'good effects' and 'bad effects' – and then decide which ones affect you where you live. Add any others you can think of.

- aircraft noise over my neighbourhood
- heavy traffic in my town
- tourists visiting local sites and beauty spots
- part-time jobs available in the holiday season
- busy town centre, with a mix of shops, restaurants, cinemas and bars
- crowded public transport
- new buildings, such as hotels
- good transport links – lots of buses and trains, running late at night and at weekends
- pollution by aeroplanes, coaches and cars.

The benefits and costs of tourism

Most countries that are now popular with tourists did not plan their tourism industry. It developed because people offered holidays there, and tourists wanted to visit. While the industry can bring benefits, it can also bring problems – some of which might not have been expected.

A Tourists cause litter and dirt. We have to spend money cleaning up after them.

B The hotels and restaurants we build for tourists provide jobs for hundreds of people – waiters, kitchen staff, cleaners and so on.

C Tourism means extra traffic. The aeroplanes, coaches, cars and taxis cause noise and pollution, which makes the air unhealthy for our children to breathe.

D Tourism brings extra money to our country, which the government can spend on things like health care and schools.

E The scenery is ruined when land is used to build hotels, apartment blocks and nightclubs.

F Tourists don't respect our customs. People dress on the beach and in the street in a way that we find offensive.

G Our ancient sites are being ruined by thousands of people walking on them.

H Because of tourism, the government has provided more art galleries and museums for everyone to enjoy.

I Local people who want jobs in the tourist industry are willing to learn foreign languages and new skills.

J Young people get dissatisfied with their lives when they see how much money the foreign tourists have.

Your country sure is beautiful.

K We have terrible water shortages because of the swimming pools built for tourists.

L Tourists cause trouble in the bars and nightclubs.

M We have a beautiful country and we are proud that people want to visit us and find out more about us.

N Everyone is better off through tourism because all businesses get extra customers – ice-cream sellers, taxi drivers, market-stall holders – everyone.

O Local people cannot enjoy the tourist facilities because they are too expensive.

P Many local people can now buy all sorts of things they could not afford before the tourists came.

Activity

In pairs, look at the opinions (A–P) from people who live in tourist destinations.

1 Draw a chart like the one below and sort the opinions into two lists:

Benefits of tourism	Problems of tourism

2 Choose two opinions you strongly agree or disagree with, and explain why.

3 In what ways might some of the problems be reduced? Think about:

a) what tourists could do
b) what the governments of the countries could do.

4 On balance, do you think tourism is good for a country?

85

How would you develop tourism in Myssia?

Imagine a small country on the edge of the Pacific Ocean – let's call it Myssia. On one side is the ocean and on the other high mountains, which cut it off from other countries. Between the mountains and the ocean is a large, mainly flat plain. There is no airport, and only one small port, where ships call.

The land is very beautiful. There are long empty beaches lapped by crystal-clear water. Great shoals of colourful tropical fish live around a coral reef. In the mountains there are rare birds and animals. Myssia has an ancient culture – there are stone circles and huge sculptures of figures all over the country that are not found anywhere else in the world. Religion is very strong and there are temples and shrines.

Only a few thousand people live in Myssia. Their huts and small houses contain barely any furniture. They have few possessions and do not use money a great deal, often bartering* goods with each other. They mostly earn their living in three ways:

- farming – grazing their animals on the plains, although the grassland is not rich and grows just enough crops and vegetables to support the rest of the population
- fishing
- diving for pearls on the reefs just offshore.

Some inhabitants make craft goods, such as baskets and wood and stone carvings, which they trade for manufactured goods.

The one big drawback in Myssia is that there is not enough work for young people. Each year, many of them leave to search for work in the big cities in the nearby countries. Those who return talk about all the things people have in these other countries, such as televisions, MP3 players and motorcycles. Some of the inhabitants would like to have similar things themselves, as well as to develop their education and health services.

* This is exchanging goods or services for other goods or services, without using any money.

Responsible tourism

Some tour operators now offer holidays based on the idea of responsible tourism which:

- protects the environment, e.g. not littering or damaging coral reefs
- makes sure money goes to local people by using local shops and restaurants, and employing local guides
- respects local culture, e.g. dressing in a way that does not offend religious beliefs or local custom
- does not waste natural resources like water, which is often in short supply in hot countries
- keeps pollution to a minimum, e.g. noise, waste disposal and traffic congestion.

Activity

Work in small groups and use ideas from pages 82–5 to do this activity.

1 Imagine you are a tour operator (someone who sells holidays to people). What would you put in a holiday resort on Myssia to attract visitors? These could include things to see and do, trips, and so on.

2 Design an advert tempting tourists to Myssia, assuming that the things you suggested in question 1 were actually carried out.

3 What do you think could be the effects of this development on the following groups?

- young people
- elders who have lived in Myssia all their life
- families with young children
- farmers and fishermen
- religious leaders

4 Use the 'Responsible tourism' box to help you answer these questions:

a) What do you think would be the worst effects of development?

b) What do you think would be the best effects?

c) How could you avoid the worst effects?

d) How could you make sure the people of Myssia benefited?

Reflection

How well do you think you're doing?
Think back over the work you have done in Section 3.

Skills

- Draw a chart like the one below, and give yourself a grade from 1 to 5, where 1 is the lowest and 5 is the highest.
- Give evidence for your score and say how you could improve your skills.

How well can you … ?	1	2	3	4	5	Evidence for your score?	How can you improve?
express your opinions							
explain and justify your opinions							
listen to other people's opinions							
see things from another person's point of view							
explain someone else's views, even if you disagree with them							
carry out research on the internet							
present your findings to other people							

Understanding

- Complete the following sentences:
  'Countries in the world are interdependent because … '
  'Children's rights can be protected by …'
- What does it mean if a product has this logo?

- Talk to another pupil and discuss what you think was the most important thing you learned in this section.

Glossary

active citizen someone who wants to change things for the better, who is prepared to argue for and take action to change things or resist an unwanted change

campaign the activities that candidates and their supporters undertake to persuade people to vote for them

charity the giving of help, money or food to those in need, or an organisation set up to provide these things

child labour children who work to help support their families or themselves

civil liberties the right to freedom of speech and action

community a group of people who live near each other in a local area; a group of people who share common beliefs or ways of life

councillor a person who is elected to sit on a council

culture things we learn from our upbringing and the people around us including traditions, beliefs and values that influence our behaviour

democracy a system of government where people regularly elect their leaders and have a say in the way a country is governed

discrimination treating someone unfairly because of your prejudices

election a way of choosing someone for a particular position by voting

fairness treating people in a just, unbiased way

global worldwide

global interdependence the way countries depend on each other, through trade for their survival and well-being

government the group of people who run a country

human rights rights that are held to belong to any person. The United Nations Universal Declaration of Human Rights, 1948, sets out a full list of the rights that all people should have. These include the right to life, liberty, education, freedom of movement and equality before the law.

identity who somebody is; the view people have of themselves which often includes the group(s) to which they belong, such as ethnic or religious group

image the way a person, a country, a place or an event is represented: for example, by a picture, a diagram or a description

intolerance refusing to accept that other people have a right to be different; not tolerating other people's views, beliefs and behaviour

law a rule that has the backing of the government

opinion what somebody thinks about a particular issue; not fact

participation taking part in the life of a school, community or organisation, involving individuals meeting and working with each other

poverty where a person or a community lack the essentials for a minimum standard of well-being and life

prejudice opinions that we form without knowing all the facts or much information

punishment a penalty for a crime or offence: for example, school detention, imprisonment

responsibility recognising what you owe to other people in your community; acting towards other people in a caring or thoughtful way; being accountable for your own actions

rights claims and privileges we expect to have, how we want to be treated by others

rules the code of behaviour that is laid down in a group or organisation, which everyone is expected to obey

stereotype a description of groups of people who have something in common, such as their religion, their age, their sex or their nationality. The description is applied to everyone in the group and ignores individual differences between people

Index